DICK HAMILTON'S FORTUNE

OR

THE STIRRING DOINGS OF A MILLIONAIRE'S SON

HOWARD R. GARIS

[ZHINGOORA BOOKS]

This edition is published by
Zhingoora Books.

PREFACE

My Dear Boys:

Allow me to introduce to you my friend, Dick Hamilton.

Dick, here are the boys, thousands of them.

Boys, here is Dick Hamilton.

Now I hope you will shake hands and become good friends; not doing as I have sometimes seen boys do, when introduced, hang back and size each other up, as if distrusting each other.

Go right up to Dick, get a good grip on his hand, and squeeze for all you're worth. I'll wager you can't make him cry "enough!"

I know he will like you, boys, and I hope you'll like Dick. He's a fine fellow, if I do say it myself, for I'm a sort of relation to him. He's got lots of money, but he uses it in the right way, to help his friends, and it doesn't keep him from getting into trouble.

I have endeavored to give you a story of Dick and his fortune; how he tried to fulfil the strange condition of his mother's will; how he escaped the toils of the sharper, was the target for many cranks, as well as well-meaning persons; how he aided the "fresh-air kids," and, finally, when the gold mines had failed, how he worked hard to escape the clutches of his uncle Ezra.

As you have taken kindly to some of the other books I have been privileged to write for you, I hope you will like this one; and now, if you have read thus far, you may turn the pages and find out what Dick had to do in order to retain his millions.

Yours sincerely,
Howard R. Garis.

CONTENTS.

CHAPTER I

DICK IS IN A HURRY

"Here comes Dick Hamilton!" exclaimed a flashily-dressed youth to his companion, no less gaily attired, as the two stood in front of a building from which sounded a peculiar clicking noise.

"So it is, Guy," was the answer. "Let's get him into a game. Maybe I can win a little money. I need it, for I'm nearly dead broke."

"I thought you always had all the cash you wanted, Simon," remarked Guy Fletcher, with something like a sneer in his voice. "I know I loaned you some the other day."

"Do you think that lasted until now?" inquired Simon Scardale, glancing down at his patent leather shoes. "I'm short of ready money now, and if we can get your friend Hamilton into a game of billiards I think I can beat him."

"He's no friend of mine," returned Guy, with a short laugh. "He isn't my kind, even if his father is a millionaire."

"That's the main reason why you ought to cultivate his acquaintance," returned Simon. "It pays to keep in with such fellows. But here he is. Let me do the talking. You needn't play if you don't want to."

The two boys, who in spite of their fine clothes, did not have an air of good breeding, watched the approach of Dick Hamilton as he sauntered down the main street of the town that pleasant afternoon late in June.

Dick was a boy a little above the average height, well built, with curling brown hair and eyes of the same hue. The eyes were bright and clear, and, when he looked at you they seemed to glint like moss agates, as some of his friends used to say.

"And you ought to see them when he's excited," one of Dick's acquaintances once remarked. "His eyes sparkle and seem to look right through you."

It needed but a glance to see that Dick was well dressed, with that careless air of studied negligence which so marks the person accustomed to fine raiment. Dick wore his garments as if he was "used to them and not dressed up," as Fred Murdock remarked. There was that about him which at once proclaimed him for what he was—the son of a very wealthy man, for his father, Mortimer Hamilton, counted his fortune in the millions.

As Dick came opposite the place whence issued that peculiar sound, produced by ivory balls hitting against one another, he was hailed by Simon Scardale.

"I say, Dick, come in and have a little game of billiards?"

Dick paused and looked at the speaker with a quizzical glance.

"Who's going to play?" he asked.

"Why—er—I—am—for one," replied Simon. And maybe Guy, here, will take a cue. I'll bet I can beat you, and I'll give you twenty-five points to start with. I'll bet you ten dollars——"

"No, thanks," answered Dick, in rather languid tones, but the sparkle in his brown eyes showed there was more spirit in the words than at first might be apparent. "I don't believe I care to play."

"Afraid I'll beat you!" exclaimed Simon, with a sneer.

"You were very far from doing that the last time you played at my house," retorted Dick, quickly.

"Oh, well, that—er—that was on a table you were used to, and——"

"He's worried about losing the money!" interrupted Guy Fletcher. "Come on, Simon, I'll play you. I'm not afraid of ten dollars, even if my father isn't quite as wealthy as his."

As a matter of fact Guy's father was very far from being as well off as Mr. Hamilton, but Guy took upon himself as much importance, and gave himself as many airs, as though his parent was a multi-millionaire.

"Hold on!" exclaimed Dick sharply, straightening up and thrusting his hands in the pockets of his well-fitting coat. "Now don't you fellows get any wrong notions into your heads. Go a little slow. You asked me to come into a public billiard-room and play a game with you. I——"

"Yes, and you refused because you're afraid!" retorted Guy.

"That's where you're wrong," replied Dick coolly. "I refused because, in the first place, I don't play billiards in a public resort like this. I like the game, but I have a fine table at home, and I see no reason why I should waste my time hanging around in a place that's thick with tobacco smoke, and where the language isn't the most polite, not to put it too strong. Besides, the tables are in such poor condition that——"

"Oh, so you've turned Miss Nancy!" exclaimed Simon, with a mean smirk.

"If you think so just come up to my gymnasium and put on the boxing gloves with me," invited Dick with a meaning smile; but Simon knew better than to accept. He had once boxed a friendly round with Dick and had been sore for a week afterward, for Simon was "soft."

"Another reason," continued Dick, "is that I never gamble, whether it's over a game of billiards or something else. I don't believe it's right. It isn't a question of money at all. In fact, if you need a little cash, I don't mind lending it to you. But I'll not gamble for it.

"However," went on the wealthy youth, "don't let me stand in the way of you two having a good time. 'Every one to their notion,' as the old lady said when she kissed the cow," and Dick laughed.

"What's the cow got to do with it?" inquired Simon, who did not see the point of Dick's joke.

"Afraid," murmured Guy, but so low that Dick did not hear him.

"The cow," retorted Dick, with a glance at Simon, "is a second cousin to the one that jumped over the moon. But, aside from all this," he continued, more seriously, "if I did feel like playing billiards with you in there, I couldn't do it this afternoon, for I promised my father I'd be home early. He has an appointment with me—a very important one—and I'm in a hurry to keep it."

"Didn't look so, by the way you were walking along the street a moment ago," sneered Simon.

"I was just looking at some new fishing tackle in White's window," answered Dick. "I have my horse tied in front of the post-office, and I guess you know he goes fast enough to take me home in a hurry. Now I think I'll say ta-ta, and get along. Try to work some one else into your billiard game," and, with a nod that had in it not the least sign of displeasure, in spite of his firm words, Dick turned and walked off.

"Well, if he ain't the limit!" ejaculated Guy. "He makes me tired. Come on in, I'll play you a game; but not for ten dollars. Dad growled the other day because I asked him for money, and I've got to go slow."

"I wish I'd taken him at his word and borrowed about twenty-five dollars from him," remarked Simon, as he followed Guy into the billiard-room.

Meanwhile Dick had reached the post-office, where his horse, a handsome bay of fine spirit, but gentle disposition, was waiting him. The animal whinnied with pleasure as the lad came up, and when he patted the black muzzle, the horse showed every evidence of delight.

"I wonder if they think I can't get home in a hurry on you, Rex?" asked Dick, as he loosened the strap and vaulted into the saddle. "Come on, now, show 'em how you can go!"

The splendid animal was off like a shot, many persons in the street turning to look at the pleasing picture the well-built youth made on his handsome steed. Past the billiard parlor Dick rode at a fast pace, and several youths inside hurried to the door.

"There he goes," remarked Simon, with a sneer. "I'd like to take some of the starch out of him."

"Who?" inquired another player, chalking his cue.

"Dick Hamilton."

"He hasn't any starch in him," was the answer. "He's one of the best fellows in the world. One of the very few who has not been spoiled by their father's wealth. You don't know Dick Hamilton, or you wouldn't say he's stiff or proud."

"We don't want to know him," put in Guy.

"Well, I'd be proud to," went on the player at the next table. "He isn't in my class, or, rather, I'm not in his, but he always bows pleasantly and speaks to me every time we meet. He's a real sport, he is. None of your tin-horn variety."

Through the main street of the town Dick rode, waving his hand now and then to acquaintances who saluted him. To some he called out cheery words of greeting, and to several elderly men he bowed respectfully.

As Dick turned out of the main thoroughfare into one that led to the handsome mansion where he and his father lived, he came in sight of a spectacle that made him pause. It was a rattletrap of a wagon, drawn by a horse that seemed as much in danger of falling apart as did the vehicle. In the wagon was a miscellaneous collection of scrap iron, broken pipes, pieces of stoves, fractured pulleys and bent shafting mingling in a confused mass. On the seat sat a pleasant-faced, bright-looking youth, about Dick's age, and nearly of his size.

"Hello, Henry!" called Dick. "What in the world have you got there?"

"Scrap iron, scrap wagon and a scrap horse," replied Henry Darby, with a grin.

"What are you doing?"

"Well, I'm in a sort of new venture," was the answer. "I'm collecting old iron, wherever I can find it, and selling it again. I bought up a lot out in the country, and I hired this rig to get it back to town with; only I'm afraid I'm not going to arrive."

"What's the matter?"

"Why, this horse—if you can call such an animal a dignified name like that—has the heaves, a spavin, spring-halt, blind-staggers, and a few other things. It got tired a few minutes ago, and went on a strike. I'm afraid to do anything to it to make it go for fear it'll fall apart right here in the road."

Dick, who had brought his steed to a stop, laughed heartily.

"Well, you are in a fix," he said. "But I don't understand about this old iron business."

"I've got to do something to make a living," answered Henry Darby, who seemed confused about something. "I have been doing it on a small scale for quite a while. Now I'm trying to branch out a bit. There's money in old iron, if I could sell enough of it. But I don't see how I'm going to get this load home. You might lend me your horse," he added with a laugh; for in spite of the poverty of Henry Darby, and the wealth of Dick Hamilton, the two boys were good friends.

"I'm sorry I can't do that, Henry," said Dick; and his voice showed that he was sincere. "The fact is, I'm in a hurry to get home. When I went out this morning father told me to be sure to be in at three o'clock, as he had something important to tell me."

"Maybe he's going to reduce your allowance," suggested Henry, with a laugh.

"No, I can't imagine what it is," and Dick spoke soberly "But that it's important I know by the way he acted. Otherwise I'd lend you my horse to pull that load back with. I'll tell you what I'll do, however. As soon as I get home I'll send one of the grooms out here with one of the work horses. They'll think that load is a feather. But now I am in a hurry, so I must gallop on. It won't do to keep dad waiting, especially when he laid so much stress on my being home on time."

"Oh, don't trouble about a horse. I guess I can get this—this animal to go after a while," and Henry laughed; for he was of a happy disposition, and trouble rolled away from him "like water off a duck's back," as he used to say.

"But it's no trouble at all," insisted Dick. "You wait here and I'll send a man back with a horse. You can drive him home to-morrow, or to-night, if you like."

"All right. It's very kind of you," said Henry, but Dick did not stay to listen to the thanks before he had called to Rex, under whose flying feet the dust of the road arose in a cloud.

"He must be in a hurry to ride like that," thought Henry, as he tried to lead on his apology for a horse. "I wonder what it is that his father is going to tell him? It must be about money I guess, for Mr. Hamilton has so much he doesn't know what to do with all of it."

Dick was also wondering, as he galloped along, what the important matter might be that his parent was to speak to him about. He only had a hint of it in what Mr. Hamilton had said that morning.

"This is your birthday," Dick's father had remarked, when he and his son were at breakfast in the Hamilton mansion. "I wish you many happy returns, and I will add that I have something very important to say to you this afternoon—something that may have a great influence on your future life. I will meet you here in the library at three o'clock, and communicate to you certain portions of your dear mother's will."

For a moment emotion had overcame Mr. Hamilton, for his wife, of whom he had been devotedly fond, though dead some years, was ever a living memory to him. Dick's eyes filled with tears as he recalled the sweet-faced woman to whom he had lisped "mother," for he was only a small chap when she died.

"So, if you will be here on time, Dick," his father finally went on, "I will read to you an important document, in accordance with your mother's final instructions. Now don't be late. I am a busy man, and if I make an appointment for a certain time, I like the other fellow to be there also," and he smiled at his son.

"I'll be there, father," promised Dick.

So now he was hurrying on to keep his appointment. His home was about two miles from the town of Hamilton Corners, in one of our eastern states, the place having been named in honor of Mr. Hamilton, who, as will be told later, was at the head of many industries that gave the town its importance.

"I wonder what it can all be about?" mused Dick, as he turned his horse into the driveway that led to the mansion.

In a vague way he knew that his mother had been very wealthy in her own right; almost as wealthy as Mr. Hamilton, who was many times a millionaire. But Dick had no idea of the provisions of his mother's will. He had often heard his father speak of what a wise and far-seeing woman Mrs. Hamilton was; but Dick, who was a healthy, happy youth, fond of all kinds of sports, had not up to this time given much thought to the future.

Now, to-day, he was to be given a glimpse into it, and he was not a little sobered by the thoughts of the coming interview.

CHAPTER II

A STRANGE WILL

"Well, I'm glad to see you are on time, Dick," said Mr. Hamilton, as his son, having left Rex at the stables, and sent one of the grooms on a horse to the aid of Henry, entered the handsome library. "Right to the minute. That is what I like to see. It speaks well for what we have in hand."

Dick had never known his father to be quite so solemn save on one former occasion, and that was the dreadful day when the house was dark and in confusion, followed by a strange stillness, and then his loving mother was seen no more. She had gone away—somewhere—he did not understand where until long afterward, and it now made him a little sad to recall the scene.

But his thoughts were interrupted by a sudden rush of feet, and a big bulldog, with fore legs arched almost grotesquely, and with two big teeth showing from under the upper lip, leaped joyously upon him.

"Grit, old boy!" exclaimed Dick, as he caressed the brute, handsome in its very ugliness, a dog, the look of which impressed strangers with fear as to its temper, but which, to all friends, was as gentle as a kitten. It was a fine specimen of the bulldog, of good stock and very valuable.

"My son," began Mr. Hamilton, as he drew from his pocket a folded paper, "I asked you to meet me here to-day to listen to some of the provisions of your dear, departed mother's will. I have a copy of it, the original being on file at the court house according to law. Soon after you were born she had it drawn up, and, having told me the nature of it, asked if I was satisfied. I told her I was, absolutely.

"You may have heard, in a general way, that your mother was very wealthy in her own right. She was, more so than you have any idea of, perhaps. It is not necessary to go into figures now, but sufficient to say that her fortune was a very large one, and that it can be counted in the millions. Part of it was left her by her father, and the rest accumulated through wise investments.

"In fact, your mother was a great believer in wise and paying investments, as you will see. She was worried lest her only son, when he grew up, would not appreciate the value of money; nor understand how much good can be done with it.

"Therefore, in order to make sure that you would not do as so many rich youths have done—wasted the wealth left to them—she has seen fit to make certain provisions and restrictions. You are to inherit her great wealth—if you fulfill these conditions."

"What are they?" asked Dick, who was not a little impressed by what his father had said. "Down, Grit, down," he commanded gently, for the dog was trying to clamber all over its master, so glad was it to see Dick. "Down, Grit," and the noble animal obeyed, crouching at the youth's feet, but ever keeping a watchful eye on his face, ready to begin the demonstration again at the first sign of encouragement.

"You are to inherit your mother's wealth on this condition, among others," went on Mr. Hamilton. "Beginning with this, your birthday, which is the time she set, you are to be supplied with a large amount of cash. You are to be allowed to spend it as you please, when you please, and for what you please, subject, of course, to certain common-sense restrictions, of which I am to be the judge."

"Does that mean I'll have all the money I want to spend just as I please?" asked Dick joyfully.

"Practically so. But here is the restriction: You are required to make, within one year from date, one wise and paying investment with some of the money you spend. It may be a large one or it may be a small one, but at the end of the year it must show a respectable profit."

"And if it doesn't?"

"Then you will lose considerable," went on Mr. Hamilton. "In the event of your failure to make such an investment within twelve months your mother's fortune will be tied up so that you can not touch it, or derive any benefit from it, for a certain period, which will be disclosed later."

"Does that mean I will have to be—be poor?"

"Well, not exactly poor, but you will have to put up with a good deal less than you have now. You see, your mother's idea was to have you avoid the pitfalls and snares into which fall many wealthy youths with millionaire parents. She wanted to make you appreciate the value of money, to know how to spend it, and to learn, above everything else, that money begets money.

"That is why she made such a peculiar will, and, I think, she did wisely. So, for a year, at least, you are to live as do other millionaires' sons who are older. In fact, you are to have more money to spend than you ever had before, for, though I have been liberal with you, I wanted you to have something still better to look forward to. So, now, your fortune is your own to make.

"If you devote some of the money you are to have to a wise and paying investment, you will, comparatively soon, come into possession of your mother's vast wealth, though, of course, the executors of the will, of whom I am one, are to have certain control over you. You have twelve months from to-day in which to make your try, Dick, my boy."

"A year to make money out of money. But how, father? I have no knowledge of business."

"That is just it. You must gain some knowledge of business or you will never be able to take care of your fortune. That is one reason your mother made such a will. I need not say I hope you will be successful. I shall aid you all I can, but I would rather you relied on yourself. I had to do it when I was your age, and I see no reason why you should not take some responsibility."

"Are these all the restrictions?" asked Dick, his mind somewhat confused by the sudden news.

"No, not all. There are a number of provisions of the will, governing your future life, aside from the matter of the investment. I will not read them to you now, but as soon as the occasion arises you will be made acquainted with them."

"And can I start in and have the money at once? I know a lot of things I want." Dick was walking about excitedly. He had visions of a big automobile and a fine motor boat, two things his father, up to the present, had not allowed him to own.

"One of the provisions of the will," went on Mr. Hamilton, "is that on this date there is to be placed a large sum to your credit in the local national bank, of which you know I am president. You will be given a check book and allowed to draw upon it as you please, subject, as I said before, to certain reasonable restrictions on my part."

"Where is the check book?" asked Dick. "I've always wanted to have one."

"Not so fast," continued his father, with a smile. "You must first go to the bank and be identified by the proper officials, and also leave your signature there. Then you shall have the check book, Dick. But there is another matter," and Mr. Hamilton turned to the second page of the document in his hand.

Dick's heart sank. Perhaps, after all, he was not to have the wealth with which his imagination was already building fairy castles in the air.

"In case you fail to make this paying investment," went on Mr. Hamilton, "not only do you lose control of the money for a long time, but you have to undergo a sort of penance. It is this. You will have to go and live with your Uncle Ezra Larabee at Dankville——"

"Uncle Ezra!" exclaimed Dick, and his face fell.

"Yes, your Uncle Ezra and Aunt Samanthy. You will have to remain in their charge for a certain period and attend any boarding school they may select for you. That is done to teach you the value of money, and I think, from what I know of your Uncle Ezra, it will be a good place to learn," and Mr. Hamilton smiled rather grimly.

"In order that you may fully appreciate the situation, your mother has provided," proceeded Dick's father, "that you are to spend a week with your Uncle Ezra, beginning to-morrow. Her idea was that you should get better acquainted with her only brother, who, as you may have heard, is quite well off, and one of the wisest men in the matter of money I ever met. He is very conservative about investments, but he makes them pay. Your dear mother thought it would be a good school for you, and I have no doubt but what you will see that for yourself if you spend a week with him. If you should not be able, in the year, to make the paying investment, you will, of course, pass under the control of Mr. Larabee.

"I think I have now told you enough for the present. As I said, there are other provisions in the will regarding you, but we can discuss them when the time comes. I have written to your uncle, and he expects you to-morrow.

"Now, Dick, my son, having gotten this somewhat sad business over—for it makes me sad to recall your dear mother, and the careful way she made provision that you should grow up to be a wise and good man—I think we will have a little lunch. I am hungry and I think you are, so I arranged a little birthday dinner for you."

Mr. Hamilton led the way to the large dining room, where, upon the mahogany table, cut glass and silver sparkled in profusion. There were places for two and, as soon as father and son entered, a solemn butler rang a chiming bell, and servants brought in a dainty but bountiful meal.

"Roast duck!" exclaimed Dick, as he caught sight of it. "That's like you, dad, to remember how fond I am of it. And I'll bet he's ordered frozen pudding for dessert;

hasn't he, Mary?" turning to the smiling maid who was arranging some dishes on the sideboard.

"That he has, Master Dick," was the reply.

"Well, I thought I'd give you a good meal before you went to Uncle Ezra's house," said Mr. Hamilton, with a queer smile. "You may not get—But there, Dick, I wish you all the luck in the world, and may we both be as happy on your next birthday," and Mr. Hamilton stood up and gravely shook hands with his son.

"Um," murmured Dick. "Maybe I'll be at Uncle Ezra's a year from now—if I don't make that paying investment. I wonder what sort of a place he has, anyhow? Well, there's no use worrying now. I must take some of that roast duck while it's hot," and he began to investigate his well-filled plate with no little interest.

"You leave for your uncle's on the eight o'clock train to-morrow morning," said Mr. Hamilton. "Have your things all packed to-night, and don't be late, for your uncle is a very particular man—a—very—particular—man," and again that grim smile came over Mr. Hamilton's face; a smile which puzzled Dick. But he was to know the meaning of it soon enough.

CHAPTER III

UNCLE EZRA THREATENS

Dick had not paid a visit to his Uncle Ezra since he could remember. He dimly recalled being there when a small boy, and had a hazy memory of a fine big house, but very gloomy, standing in the midst of large grounds that seemed more like a cemetery than anything else. Of his uncle and aunt he had but a faint recollection, and when he stood on the depot platform the next morning, waiting for his train, he was in no very happy frame of mind.

For Dick liked fun, and jolly companions, and did not relish being sent off to visit relatives who were almost strangers to him, even though Mr. Larabee was his mother's only brother.

"I don't fancy I'm going to have a very good time," mused the youth, as the train was whizzing him along toward Dankville. "Still, I'm going to fulfill the conditions of the will as far as I can. Make a paying investment, eh? I wonder if I can do it? But, of course, I can. I'll buy some building lots, stocks or bonds, and sell 'em at a profit. I'll do it as soon as I get home,and then I'll not have to worry about the matter any more," he added lightly, as if making money was the easiest thing in the world.

Dankville was a country village about a hundred miles from Hamilton Corners. When Dick alighted at the station he looked around in some surprise. The place seemed to be absolutely deserted. There was no one in sight but the station agent, and, as soon as the train pulled out, he disappeared into his office.

"Not a very pleasant reception," mused Dick, as he sat down on the upturned end of his dress-suit case. "Not exactly a brass band out to meet me. I wonder how I get to Uncle Ezra's place? Guess I'll ask the man."

He started toward the ticket office, but, as he approached it, he saw a carriage driving up to the platform. In the vehicle sat an elderly man with a little tuft of white chin whiskers, which moved to and fro in a curious manner every time he spoke to the horse, which was frequently necessary, as the animal seemed to need much urging to induce it to continue its journey.

"Whoa!" exclaimed the man, though there was no occasion for the command, as the horse was glad enough to stop. "Are you Richard Hamilton, son of Mortimer Hamilton?"

"I'm Dick. Are you Uncle Ezra?"

"Dick!" fairly snorted the elderly man. "You're Richard, that's what you were christened and that's what you must be called! I can't abide nicknames and I won't have 'em. You're Richard, do you hear?"

"Yes, sir," answered Dick, meekly enough, though there was an angry light in his eyes.

"Now, then, Richard, you've come to visit us for a certain purpose," went on his uncle. "What it is we needn't discuss now. The train was a little ahead of time or I'd been here sooner." Mr. Larabee did not seem to think that he might be a little late. "I always make it a point to be on time," he added. "Now, jump in. Your aunt has a meal ready and she musn't be kept waiting. I want you to understand from the start that everything is done on time in my house. We rise at a certain hour, and we have our meals at certain hours. Folks that come to see us have to do as we do or they don't get any meals. I hope you understand that."

"Yes, sir," replied Dick, his heart sinking down deeper than ever. It was worse than he had thought. Still the idea of a meal, after his long ride, seemed good.

Mr. Larabee's fine country home was considered one of the best places in that part of the state. There was not a crooked fence on it, the gravel walks were as trim as though no one had ever stepped on their surface, and the grass was always cut to a certain length. The house was always painted at a certain time of the year, as were also the barns, and the place looked almost like a picture in a book.

In fact, Mr. Larabee's neighbors used to say he never took any pleasure in it, as he was always so busy looking to see if a stick or a stone had not become misplaced, or if the paint on the house or barn was not chipping off.

"So this is Nephew Richard, is it?" asked a small, prim, rather thin-faced woman, as she came to the door when the carriage containing Dick and his uncle drove up the path. "I'm glad to see you, Nephew Richard," she went on, extending a cold and clammy hand, and giving Dick a little peck that seemed more like a nip from a bird than a kiss.

"Is dinner ready?" asked Mr. Larabee.

"You know it is, Ezra," replied his wife. "I'll serve it as soon as you put the horse up. Come in, Nephew Richard, but be sure and wipe your feet."

She watched Dick while he scraped off an invisible quantity of dust from his shoes that had scarcely touched the ground that morning. After giving them what he thought was a good polishing on the mat, he started to enter the front hall.

"Wait!" almost screamed his aunt. "There's a little mud on that left heel!"

Dick obligingly gave it another scrape on the mat and started in.

"One moment, Nephew Richard," said Mrs. Larabee, in almost imploring accents. "Let me wipe your satchel off before you go in. I'm afraid it's dusty from the drive, and I can't bear dust in my house."

She kept Dick waiting on the front steps while she went in and got a cloth, with which she carefully wiped off the dress-suit case, though Dick did not see how there could be any dust on it, as it had been covered with the lap robe all the way.

"Now you may come in," Aunt Samantha said, as graciously as was possible. "Welcome to The Firs. We call our place The Firs," she went on, "because there are so many fir trees around it. It makes it dark and keeps the flies out."

It certainly made it dark, for as Dick entered the hall he could hardly see, and had to proceed by the sense of feeling.

"We never open this part of the house, except for company," Mrs. Larabee went on. "Ezra and I use the back door, as it saves wear and tear. Now, if you'll come with me, I'll show you to your room and you can take off your good clothes and put on a rough suit."

"I haven't any rougher suit than this," said Dick, looking at the garments he wore. "I've got another suit in the case, but it's newer than this."

"Mercy, child!" exclaimed his aunt. "Would you wear such clothes around every day?"

"I always have," replied Dick simply.

"Well, I never heard tell the like of that! What does your father—but, there, I forgot. I know Mortimer Hamilton. He doesn't care how he throws money away!"

"My father never throws money away!" exclaimed Dick, always ready to champion his parent. "He thinks it pays to buy good clothes, as they wear better than cheap ones."

"Such wastefulness," sighed the aunt, as she led the way upstairs. "But it's no use talking. However, if you come to live here——"

She did not finish the sentence, but Dick registered a mental vow that it would be a long day before he would voluntarily come to live at The Firs.

He was shown into a small room, plainly furnished, containing a small cot bed.

"As you are only to stay a week, I thought it would make less work for me if you had this room," said Mrs. Larabee. "It used to be the servant's, but I don't keep any now. They are too expensive. Now be very careful. Always take your shoes off when you come upstairs, as I can't be always cleaning and dusting. Don't throw your things around, and keep the shutters closed so the flies won't get in. When you are ready come down to dinner."

"Well, if this doesn't get me!" exclaimed Dick, when his aunt had left him alone and he had dropped down on the edge of the cot. "This certainly is the limit. If I didn't know differently I'd say Uncle Ezra had lost all his money. I guess he's got it salted down and hates to take it out of the brine. Well, I'll see what they have for dinner before I make up my mind any further."

The meal, though plain, was good, and to a boy with Dick's appetite, nothing came amiss. But it was small pleasure to dine when two pair of eyes were almost constantly watching him.

"Don't get any of the gravy on the table cloth," cautioned Mrs. Larabee. "It was clean this week, and I don't want to have to put another one on before Sunday."

Dick felt a guilty flush come over his face as he saw that he had dropped a small piece of butter on the cloth. But he thought it wisest to say nothing.

"Aren't you going to eat that crust of bread?" asked his uncle, as Dick laid aside a portion that was burned black.

"It's a little too—too brown," replied the boy, who did not fancy burned bread.

"That makes it all the better," said Mr. Larabee. "Bread should be well cooked to be digestible. Always eat your crusts. 'Sinful waste makes woeful want,' as the proverb says. I had to eat my crusts when I was young."

Dick managed to get it down, and the meal finally came to a close. He felt considerably better after it, and when his uncle proposed a walk around the place, he was ready to accompany Mr. Larabee.

Dick found much to admire in the well-kept grounds. Several men were at work, and the manner in which they hastened with their tasks when their employer approached spoke volumes for the way in which they regarded him.

Dick paused in the stable to admire the horses, of which his uncle kept several. Without thinking he pulled a wisp of hay from a bale and offered it to one of the animals.

"Don't do that!" exclaimed his uncle sharply. "You'll scatter it all over the barn. The man has just swept the place up, and I don't like a litter of dirt around."

He stopped to pick up some pieces of hay Dick had inadvertently dropped, and looked so cross that the boy wished he had kept out of the stable.

However, Mr. Larabee seemed a bit ashamed of himself a little later, for he showed Dick where he could find some withered apples to feed to the pigs.

"Only don't scatter 'em on the ground," he cautioned. "I hate to see apples thrown about. I keep a man to look after the orchard, and I like it nice and tidy."

Now Dick was not a careless youth, but he thought this was carrying things a little too far. However, he brightened up a bit when his uncle announced that he had to leave his nephew to his own devices for a time, as he had some duties to attend to.

Dick managed to while away the afternoon looking at the sights around the place, for his uncle had a large farm, though he was wealthy enough not to need the income from it. Still he was the kind of a man who can not own the smallest bit of land without putting it to some use.

Dick looked about for a sight of some lads of his own age with whom he might become acquainted and enjoy his enforced visit to Dankville, but boys seemed a scarce article around The Firs.

He strolled back to the house, and, not seeing his aunt about, and being desirous of exploring the rather stately mansion, he started on a tour of it. Through the darkened hall he went until he came to what he thought would be the parlor. He opened the door, though it creaked on rusty hinges.

The room was so dark he could see nothing, and, having heard his father say that there were some choice oil paintings at The Firs, he opened a window to get light enough to view them. He had a hard task, as it seemed the sash and shutters had not been moved since they were built, but finally a stream of light entered the gloomy apartment, with the horse-hair furniture arranged stiffly against the wall.

Dick caught sight of a large painting and was going closer to examine it when he heard a shriek in the open doorway.

"Mercy sakes, Richard! Whatever have you done?" he heard his aunt call.

"Why, I just opened a window to let some light in, so I could see the pictures," he answered.

"Light? In this room? Why, Richard Hamilton! This room hasn't been opened in years! We never think of letting light in the parlor. The carpet might fade. Oh, Richard, I am so sorry! If I thought you would have opened a window I would have locked the door. Shut it and come out at once! Mercy sakes!"

Much abashed, Dick closed the shutters and window and walked out. His aunt ran and got a broom, with which she brushed the carpet where he had stepped, though how she could see any dust in that gloom was more than the boy could understand.

"Never, never go in there again," cautioned his aunt. "We never open that room except—for funerals."

"I guess that's all it's good for," thought Dick.

He sat around, very miserable, the remainder of the afternoon, and had little appetite for supper, which was rather a scant meal; some preserves, bread and weak tea making up the repast.

"I think I'll take a stroll to the village," remarked the youth, as he arose from the table.

"Where?" asked his aunt, as if she had not heard aright.

"To the village. I'd like to see what's going on."

"There's nothing going on," replied his uncle. "The village is five miles from here. Besides, we go to bed early, and I don't allow any one in my house, visitor or otherwise, to come in with a latch key. You'd better stay here, read some good book to improve your mind, and retire early. That's what I do, and I find it pays."

Dick groaned. He now knew the meaning of his father's queer smile.

"Then I'll walk around outside the house for a while to get some air," proposed Dick.

"I'd rather you wouldn't," came from Mr. Larabee, as he squirmed uneasily in his chair. "The gravel walks have just been raked smooth, and I hate to have 'em disturbed."

Dick did not answer, but sat in his chair silently, while his aunt cleared off the supper table. When the lamps were lighted, which was not done until it was quite dark, Mr. Larabee handed Dick a book. The boy hoped it might be some tale of adventures that would help pass away the hours, but on looking at the title he saw it was "Pilgrim's Progress."

"I guess I'll go to bed," he announced, and his aunt and uncle gave an audible sigh of relief.

The next morning Dick, without saying anything to Mr. or Mrs. Larabee, walked to the railroad station. There he sent a telegram to his father. It read:

"Dear Dad. This place is fierce. Can't I come home? Wire me quick."

He said he would wait at the station for an answer, and he was a little sorry when it came, as it meant he would have to go back to the dismal house. His father's reply was:

"Dear Dick. To fulfill the conditions you must remain a week. Do the best you can and let it be a lesson to you."

"Be a lesson to me?" mused Dick. "Oh, I see! He means I must make that investment so I won't have to come here and live."

On his return Dick entered the house at the rear door, pausing momentarily to wipe his feet. But his aunt was watching for him.

"Richard," she said severely. "They're not half clean. I can see dirt on them."

"Oh," he began, but he kept silent, and, instead of entering, turned into the orchard. There, at least, he would not be corrected. His uncle found him there a little later, as Dick was sitting idly under a tree.

"Haven't you anything to occupy yourself with?" asked Mr. Larabee severely.

"No," answered Dick. "There's no one to get up a baseball game with around here, as far as I can see."

"Boys shouldn't always be playing," commented Mr. Larabee. "You should labor to improve your mind. Why don't you read that book I gave you last night?"

"I don't care for it."

"That's the way with the rising generation. Frivolous! frivolous!"

"School has closed for the term," said Dick. "I'm done with studying, and that book looked as if it was to be studied."

"It was," replied his uncle. "It merits being well studied. But it's what I expected of you. It's the way that you have been brought up."

"I guess my father brought me up in the way he thought best," fired back Dick.

"Well, his way is very different from mine—very different," and Mr. Larabee shook his head as though to indicate that a great mistake had been made. "Then there's your mother's will," he went on. "The idea of leaving that big fortune to a boy like you. It's wicked! It's a terrible risk! A terrible risk! What a foolish woman she was! But then it's all you can expect of a woman!"

"Look here, Uncle Ezra!" exclaimed Dick, rising to his feet, his brown eyes sparkling in a dangerous way, and a red flush showing on his cheeks. "I don't want you to speak that way of my mother!"

"She was my sister, and I say she made a foolish will!" stormed the old man.

"She was my mother!" replied Dick hotly, "and I'll not have her spoken of in that way! She knew what she was doing! She was the best woman that ever lived and— and much better than you are with your ideas of what is good. You musn't speak so of her! I'll not stand it!"

"Look here, young man!" exclaimed Mr. Larabee. "I guess you forget who you're talking to."

"No, I don't!"

"I won't have such language used toward me. I say your mother made a foolish will, and I know what I'm talking about."

"If you say that again I'll—I'll—" and then Dick paused. After all this man was his mother's brother, and he knew how his parent would have gently reproved him had she been alive. The memory of her took all the hard feeling out of his heart.

"I'm sorry I spoke so hastily, Uncle Ezra," he said in a low voice. "But I can't bear to have my mother referred to in that way. I think she did what was right, and I know my father does also."

"Humph, little he knows about it," snorted Mr. Larabee. "Just you wait until you come under my care, young man, and I'll show you what's what! I'll teach you how to behave to your elders," and, in great indignation, the old man trudged off.

Dick started. He had, for the moment, forgotten that portion of his mother's will which, under certain conditions, would compel him to live with his uncle and aunt.

"Live with them?" thought the boy. "Go to a boarding school they might select? Not much! I must make some kind of a paying investment within a year, if only to escape their clutches!"

CHAPTER IV

DICK BECOMES CELEBRATED

Dick managed to live through the week at his uncle's place, but it was hard work. He was corrected from morning until night. Almost everything he did while in the house, if it was only to pick up a book in the hope of finding something to read, met with a reproof from Aunt Samantha.

"Don't do that," she would say. "You'll make the dust fly about if you disturb the books, and I can't abide dust."

If he wandered about the grounds his uncle would covertly watch him.

"Don't pick up stones to throw," Mr. Larabee would caution the lad. "You might break a window, or take the bark off my favorite apple trees. I never saw such a boy! Why can't you sit still and think? I'm sure you've got enough responsibilities hanging over you, with all that money your mother so foolishly——"

But he had the sense to stop there, for the angry flash in Dick's brown eyes warned him this was a subject he had better not mention to his nephew.

There was never a more happy boy than Dick when the week of probation was up and he could start for home.

"You are going back to that wasteful life of idleness," said his aunt, as she condescended to shake hands with him, and give him her little bird-like kiss. "I hope your visit here has done you good. You may make us a longer one—some day."

"Not if I can help it," thought Dick to himself.

"Come, now," grumbled Uncle Ezra. "I don't want to keep the horse out of the stable any longer than I can help. He might take cold and I'd have to buy some medicine. Saving money is like earning it, as I hope you'll learn, Nephew Richard. I'll teach it to you when you come under my control, as I'm sure you will, for you never can comply with the task your mother so foolishly——"

Dick's hands clinched, and it was lucky that at that moment the horse shied at a piece of paper, requiring all Mr. Larabee's attention to control him, or there might have been a renewal of the quarrel.

Dick breathed a sigh of relief as the gloomy house in the midst of the fir trees was left behind, and he gave vent to an audible exclamation of satisfaction when he was in the train and speeding away from Dankville, for even the name of the place seemed to have an unhappy influence over him.

"Well, are you glad to get back?" asked Mr. Hamilton, as he greeted his son that afternoon.

"Glad, father? Say, give me some of that money, quick! I want to make that paying investment. I never could stand it at The Firs!"

Mr. Hamilton laughed.

"Well, in spite of his queer ways, your Uncle Ezra is a man of sterling character," he said. "He is as true as steel——"

"And just about as hard," interrupted Dick, with a smile.

"But now to business," went on Mr. Hamilton. "I have deposited a large sum to your credit in our bank, and if you will come downtown with me now I'll introduce you to the cashier and see that you get a check book. Then—well, the world is before you, and it's yours—to conquer or be conquered by."

On their way to the bank father and son were greeted by many acquaintances, for Mr. Hamilton was a person of great importance in Hamilton Corners. The town was a good-sized one, situated on the shore of Lake Dunkirk, a large body of water. Mr. Hamilton, besides being president of the Hamilton National Bank, was vice-president of the Hamilton Trust Company, and owned a stone quarry, a brass foundry, large woolen mills, and a lumber concern, all in the town or its immediate vicinity.

He was also a director of the Hamilton, Dorchester and Hatfield Railroad, which ran through the town, and president of the Hamilton Trolley Company. These were all sources of Mr. Hamilton's wealth, and, as he employed many men in the various industries, which he controlled or was interested in, he was regarded as the most important man in the place.

But this did not make him overbearing in character. In fact, he was a very kind man, always ready to help the poor, and as he had begun as a poor boy and made his money by hard work, he had a great sympathy for those not so well off in this world's goods.

Dick took after his father. Though surrounded by wealth all his life, and accustomed to luxury, he was a lad of democratic spirit. He cared little for money in itself, though he appreciated what could be done with it, and he was always willing to use what he had for the benefit or pleasure of himself and his friends. He was ambitious in no small degree, and anxious to succeed in whatever he undertook.

It did not take long to get through with the formalities at the bank, and Dick's eyes sparkled when he saw the substantial balance to his credit. He took the little red check book with an air as though he had used one all his life, put it into his pocket, and, nodding to his father, walked out.

"Well," remarked Mr. Hamilton, with a little sigh, "I hope money doesn't spoil him, for he is a fine lad. But I guess the remembrance of his Uncle Ezra may have a large influence on what he does."

The first person Dick met on emerging from the bank was Henry Darby. He hailed the poorer lad.

"Well, Henry, did you get that load of iron home safe?"

"Yes, and I sold it the next day. I'm much obliged to you for sending that horse. I couldn't get the one I hired from the man, of whom I bought the iron, to go another step. I'd have been there all night if it hadn't been for you."

"That's all right. The next time I meet you in a fix like that I'll tow you home myself."

"What do you mean?"

"Why, I'm going to get an automobile."

"An automobile?" and Henry's eyes opened as wide as possible. The machines were rarely seen in Hamilton Corners.

"Yes. You see, Henry, I've come into some property, and I can spend as much money as I like—of course, not waste it. I've always wanted an auto, and I'm going to get one. I'm going for it now."

"Whew, I wish I was you," exclaimed Henry, with a sigh, as he started down the street after some more old iron he had heard was for sale.

Henry was an energetic lad, always looking for a chance to make money. He lived with his father, who was never called anything else than "Hank" Darby, and who was known as the most"shiftless" man in town. Mr. Darby was always talking of big schemes he was going to put into operation as soon as he could command the capital, but he never got the money. As a consequence he never did anything, but lived off what his son earned.

Dick had decided that his first purchase with his new wealth should be an automobile. He wanted to get a big touring car, but his father suggested that he had better start with a runabout.

"It will be less expensive if you have a smash-up learning how to run it," counseled Mr. Hamilton, and Dick wisely agreed with him.

"When I get my car I'll take a run about the country and see what sort of an investment I'll make," said Dick. "I may want to go in for real estate. There's money in that, isn't there, dad?"

"Yes, if you buy right and sell right. But that business is like everything else, you've got to learn it. However, you are your own master to a certain extent. Good luck to you."

Dick went to a neighboring city that same afternoon and purchased his runabout. He wanted to drive it home alone, but the manager of the garage sent a helper with the boy. But the man did not have much to do, for Dick was very quick and soon learned the different points. In a few days he was able to operate the machine with considerable skill, and he took a number of his boy friends for a spin in the country.

"Want to take a trip?" he called one afternoon to Simon Scardale and Guy Fletcher, whom he saw in front of the billiard room, which place they seemed to frequent very much of late.

"Sure," replied Simon. "Maybe we can get a race with some car along the road. That will be sport."

"Not for me," replied Dick quietly. "I sha'n't race until I know the car better. But come along."

In spite of their rather flashy manners, Dick liked Simon and Guy, as he did nearly everyone, in fact—for Dick Hamilton was a large-hearted youth. He accepted all his acquaintances "at one hundred cents on the dollar" until he learned to value them differently.

The three boys spent a pleasant time whirring about on the country roads.

"What do you think of that property?" asked Dick at length, pointing to a low, swampy tract.

"Why?" asked Guy. "Thinking of buying it?"

"Maybe," replied Dick. "I have a chance to get it cheap. Do you think I could sell it again?"

"Search me," answered Simon. "It looks to be good for ducks, that's all."

"It only needs draining," objected Dick. "I think it would be a good investment, and I came out here to look at it."

"Going into business?" asked Guy, with a sneer. "I thought you didn't have to work."

"Of course I'm going into business, as soon as I finish at school," said Dick, for the term at the academy, where he attended, had recently closed. "I've come into some money lately," he said modestly, for he had not spoken of his fortune to any one yet, "and I want to invest some of my spare cash."

"I'll tell you the very thing!" exclaimed Simon. "I know a stock that's bound to go up ten points in a few days."

"No stocks or bonds for me until I know a little more about them," objected Dick.

"But this is a sure thing," insisted Simon. "I got a tip on it from a friend in New York."

"I've read of too many 'sure things' going wrong," said Dick with a laugh. "I think I'll try real estate for a starter."

Simon looked a little disappointed, but he made up his mind he would try Dick again on that subject, and a strange, cunning look came into his face.

During the trip back Simon tried to learn from the millionaire's son more about his new wealth, but Dick did not give him much satisfaction. However, Simon was sharp, and by dint of skillful hints and questions learned more than Dick thought he had told. Guy, too, was much interested, and a visible change came over his manner.

Guy's father, Peter Fletcher, was president of the Hamilton Trust Company, and, though Mr. Hamilton owned most of the stock of the concern, and had only placed Mr. Fletcher at the head of the institution for business reasons, Guy gave himself as many airs as though his father owned the bank. Learning that Dick had come into possession of some wealth on his own account, though he did not know the source, Guy was somewhat inclined to toady to the youth with whom he was on more or less friendly terms.

It was two days after this, when the evening papers arrived in Hamilton Corners, that a mild sensation was created. There, on the front pages, was what purported to be a picture of Dick Hamilton, while under it was the caption, in big letters:

THE MILLIONAIRE YOUTH.

Then followed a garbled, but fairly correct, account of how Dick, through the will of his mother, had come into possession of fabulous wealth. Of course the figure was put much higher than it really was. In fact, no one but Mr. Hamilton was aware of the exact amount, but this did not stop the writer of the article from guessing at it.

Dick was described as a modern King Midas, and he was credited with sleeping in an ivory bed and eating off of gold plates and the rarest of cut glass. Nothing was said about the peculiar provisions of the will regarding the investment he was to make; but the boundless opportunities open to a youth with unlimited wealth at his disposal were all pointed out. "Well, if that isn't the limit!" exclaimed Dick, when he saw the paper. "I wonder who did it?"

Perhaps if he had asked Simon Scardale that question that youth might have been confused, but Dick never thought of it.

"It certainly is very unpleasant notoriety," remarked Mr. Hamilton, "but you'll have to put up with it. You are a sort of ward of the public now, and the newspapers think they have a proprietary interest in you. I have been through it all, and so has nearly every other person of wealth. The best way is to pay no attention to it, and to treat with courtesy any newspaper men who may wish to interview you. They have a hard enough life, and if our doings, to a certain extent, interest them, why I, for one, am willing to oblige them as far as I can. I suppose the transferring to your name of some stocks and bonds, that were your mother's, has started this piece of news. Well, you have achieved a certain degree of fame, Dick, my boy."

And Dick found this out to his cost. The article in one paper was followed by others in various journals, until Dick's wealth had been made the comment of newspaper reporters and editors in many cities. But, through it all the youth kept a level head.

CHAPTER V

DICK AIDS HENRY

"Where are you going to-day, Dick?" asked Mr. Hamilton after breakfast one morning.

"I thought of taking a run in my car. I've bought that property I was telling you about. I think it will be a good investment, and it only took five hundred dollars to secure it. I talked to the agent, and he said I was sure to be able to sell it for a thousand at the end of the year."

"Humph! Well—er—of course, you can't believe all that a real-estate agent says, Dick."

"No, of course. I'm making allowances for that, and I figure that it ought to be worth at least eight hundred a year from now. That will clear me three hundred."

"Well, you can do as you like about it. By the way, I had a visit at the bank yesterday from an agent for a motor boat concern. He said you had ordered a boat from them, and he wanted to know if it was all right."

"I did, dad. I've always wanted one. I hope you told him it was all right."

"I told him to see you about it. I have no objection to you purchasing one of the craft. Only be careful when you go out on the lake. There are sudden storms on it, and you might be in danger."

"I'll be careful, dad. I guess I'll just run over to the motor boat place in my car and see if the boat is ready to deliver. They had to order one from the factory for me."

As Dick was riding through the town at an easy pace he passed a rather dilapidated looking house, in front of which stood a youth, at the sight of whom Dick called:

"Hello, Henry! Want a ride?"

"Thanks, Dick," was Henry Darby's answer. "But I can't go."

"Why not?" asked the millionaire's son, as he brought his runabout to a stop.

"Well, I'm engaged in a little business deal, and I'm so bothered over it that I wouldn't enjoy a ride. Besides, I have to go see a man."

"What's the business about, Henry? That same old iron?"

"That's it."

"But what are you bothered about?"

"Well, the truth is I have a chance to get hold of a lot of scrap at a very low figure. But the trouble is I must pay cash for it. I looked at it the other day, and told the man I'd take it. I figured then on having the money. Now I find I haven't got it."

"Did you lose it?"

"No," and Henry spoke hesitatingly. "But you see my father had an idea he could make some money by becoming agent for a new kind of soap. He borrowed my cash and sent for a big supply; but when he got it no one would buy it. So he has it on hand, and my money is gone. Of course what I have is my father's until I'm of age, but——"

Henry stopped. In spite of the selfish and lazy character of his parent he was not going to utter any complaint against him.

"How much money do you need to buy this iron?" asked Dick, a sudden resolve coming into his mind.

"It will take fifty dollars; but it might just as well be five hundred as far as I'm concerned. I could get it together in about a month, but it's out of the question now. I'm just on my way to tell the man I can't take the iron. It's too bad, as it's a bargain, and I could easily make considerable on the deal."

While Henry was speaking Dick had drawn a little red book from his pocket, and was busily writing in it with a fountain pen. He tore out a slip of paper and handed it to his friend.

"There, Henry," he said, "if you take that to the Hamilton National Bank they'll give you cash for it."

"But what is it—I don't understand—a check for fifty dollars!" exclaimed the other youth.

"That's what it is," replied Dick smiling. "It's a present from me, Henry."

"A present! I'm sorry, but I can't take it, Dick. I'm very much obliged to you, but it wouldn't be business, you know. I don't want anything I don't earn."

"But I have lots more," insisted Dick. "In fact, I'd never miss that sum."

"I can't help it. I couldn't take it, though I thank you very much," and Henry handed back the little slip.

"Wait!" exclaimed Dick. "Will you take it as a loan, Henry?"

"A loan?"

"Yes; to be paid back—whenever you get good and ready. Do take it—as a loan."

"A loan," repeated Henry in a low tone. "Well, I might do that. But if you're in any hurry for the money you'd better not let me take it. I don't know when I can pay it back."

"That's all right. Keep it as long as you like."

"But there's another objection," said Henry, who appeared to be very conscientious about it. "You have no security for it."

"I don't need any from you, Henry."

"But it wouldn't be right to take it without security. Wait, I'll tell you what I'll do."

He hurried back into his house, to return in a few minutes with a folded paper which he handed to Dick.

"What is this?"

"That," said Henry proudly, "is my personal note for fifty dollars, payable in one month, with interest at six per cent., as security for this loan. You can have it discounted at the bank," he added with a laugh; "that is if you can get your father, or somebody with some money, to indorse it. Anyhow, it's my note. The first one I ever gave. Now you needn't worry about your money, Dick."

"I'm not worrying about it. In fact, I've got a deal of my own on hand that I expect to make some profit on. Besides, I'm going to buy a new motor boat, and I've got to go see about it. Will you come along?"

"No, indeed. I'm going to buy that old iron now," and as Dick started up his auto, Henry hurried into the house for his hat to go and complete his business transaction.

Dick rode on for about a mile, when he saw coming toward him a man in a carriage. The man held up his hand as he approached, indicating that he wanted the automobilist to stop.

"I wonder what's the matter?" thought Dick. "I can't be going so fast that I'm in danger of scaring his horse. Why, it's Mr. Bruce," as he recognized the real-estate agent of whom he had purchased the land he had been looking at with Guy and Simon one day.

"How are you?" asked Mr. Bruce. "I was just coming over to see you, Mr. Hamilton;" for he had been quite respectful to Dick since he learned of his wealth.

"To see me? What about?"

"About that land deal. In fact, I have bad news for you."

"Bad news?"

"Yes, I have just learned that they are going to put a fertilizer factory up on the property adjoining that which you bought, and yours will be valueless to sell for building lots. No one will want to live next to a fertilizer factory."

"Then it means——" faltered Dick.

"It means that your investment hasn't turned out well," went on the agent. "In fact, your land is worth less than half what you paid for it."

CHAPTER VI

A TRIP TO NEW YORK

Dick was keenly disappointed, not so much at the news of the loss of his money as he was over the fact that his first investment had proved a failure. He began to realize that it was not as easy to make money as he had supposed, even if you have a large amount to invest.

"It's too bad," continued Mr. Bruce. "Of course I did not know when I sold you the land that the factory was liable to go up near it."

"Oh, it's not your fault," replied Dick. "I guess the best thing I can do is to sell out and look for another investment. What do you think?"

"I believe I would do that. I'll sell the land for you and get the best price I can. When I first heard about it I tried to get the fertilizer concern to buy it, but they had all they wanted and stopped right next to your property. It's too bad."

"Well, it might be worse," said Dick cheerfully. "It's not going to make me poor, that's one consolation."

But, as he started up his runabout again, bidding the agent good-bye, his mind was busy with thoughts of what line he ought next to invest in so that he might fulfil the conditions of his mother's will.

"I guess I'll let real estate alone after this," he said. "It's too risky until you know what's going to be built on the property next to yours."

But the somewhat disappointing thoughts over his failure were soon dispelled when he saw the fine motor boat the firm had secured for him from the factory. It was complete in every detail, from a small whistle, worked by compressed air, to two small folding bunks in which passengers could sleep should the craft remain out on Lake Dunkirk all night.

Dick arranged to have the boat taken to the lake and floated, and, a few days later, he had the pleasure of starting it up for the initial spin. It ran at fast speed, and beat several more powerful boats.

Dick did not enjoy this pleasure all alone. He invited Guy Fletcher, Simon Scardale, Frank Bender, Fred Murdock and Chandler Norton, the latter known as "Bricktop," because of his red hair, to take a trip with him.

"This is great!" exclaimed Frank, as the boat cut through the water. "Say, Dick, you're all right, even if you are a millionaire's son and have money to burn."

"In fact, he's all the better for it," put in Guy, who had resolved to be very friendly to that fortunate youth. "Three cheers for Dick Hamilton!"

"Drop that!" commanded Dick, who disliked Guy's manner.

But the boys responded heartily, and if Guy and Simon joined in with sneers in their hearts, which did not show on their faces, they alone were aware of it.

"Here, where are you going, Frank?" asked Dick, a few minutes later as he saw one of his guests climbing out on the narrow bow of the boat.

"Watch me," replied Frank Bender, and, a moment later, he was standing on his head in his rather insecure place, his feet waving aloft in the air.

"Come back here!" cried Dick, as he slowed down the engine. "Do you want to fall off and drown?"

"No," replied Frank, as he assumed his normal position.

"But, you see, I never stood on my head on a motor boat before and I wanted to do it. I want to get all sorts of practice, for I'm going to join a circus some day, and there's no telling what stunts they may want me to do."

"Oh, you and your circus!" exclaimed "Bricktop." "You're always talking about it!"

Which was the truth, for Frank took every chance that came to him to indulge in acrobatics of one form or another. He was continually turning cart wheels, standing on his head or his hands, twisting himself into knots, from which it seemed impossible that he could ever get loose, or bending himself until he resembled an animated horse shoe. He was "as limber as an eel," the boys used to say.

"That's all right," responded the amateur circus performer, "I'll be in a show some day, with a suit of green and gold spangles, and you fellows will be paying money to see me. All except Dick. I'll give him a free pass."

"Thanks," answered Dick with a laugh, as he started the engine on full speed again.

"Say, wouldn't it be great if we could only make a trip to New York this way," remarked Fred Murdock.

"Yes, this boat would look nice traveling over dry land the best part of the way," said Dick with a smile. "If this lake only opened into a river or a canal we might do it, but it's out of the question now."

"Why don't you go in your automobile?" suggested Simon, with a curious look at Guy.

"That's so, I never thought of it," replied Dick. "I believe I will if dad will let me."

"Take us along?" asked Frank. "Maybe I could get an engagement there in one of the theatres. I can do quite a lot of turns now."

"My car's too small for this bunch," replied the millionaire's son.

"Hire a touring car; you have lots of money," spoke up Guy, with a covert sneer.

"Good idea!" exclaimed Dick, not noticing the tone of the remark. "I believe I will. Would you fellows all go?"

"Would we!" was shouted in a chorus. "Don't ask us twice," said Fred.

"All right; it's a go!" went on Dick. "I'll see about it at once."

With Dick, to think was to act shortly afterward, and that night he asked his father for permission to take a crowd of his friends to the metropolis, which could easily be reached in a day by using a swift touring car.

"Besides," added Dick, as an added reason for the permission being given, "I may hear of some investment there."

"What's the matter with the land you bought?" asked Mr. Hamilton.

"Oh, that failed," and Dick told the story of the fertilizer factory.

"Well, it's a good lesson to you, my son," was all Mr. Hamilton said by way of reproof. "No, I've no objection to you going to New York. Hire the car you wish, and be sure they supply a good driver. You're not quite capable of managing one of those ponderous machines yet. But be careful. Don't go to buying any gold bricks," and he laughed.

"No danger," replied Dick. "I've cut my eye teeth."

It was arranged that they should start in three days. Dick engaged the largest and finest car in the garage of a neighboring city, and told his friends to get ready.

"Are you going?" asked Guy of Simon, the day before that set for the trip.

"Am I? Well, you can make up your mind to that. I can see something good in this for us."

"Good? What do you mean?"

"Money, of course."

"Don't get the idea that Dick is going to distribute five-dollar gold pieces along the route, Simon."

"I'm not; but I've got a plan of my own. If this wealthy young greenhorn doesn't drop a few hundreds in New York, and if I don't get my share, I'm very much mistaken. You can just as well have some as not."

"How you going to do it?"

"That's my secret," replied Simon, with a wink. "I didn't live five years in New York for nothing. I've got some friends there who will help me. Just you wait."

"But you want to be careful. Dick is no fool, even if he is wealthy."

"Don't you worry. I know what I'm about."

The pair, who were well matched, whispered for some time together, and when they separated, Simon, with many winks, gave his companion renewed assurances that Dick's trip to New York would prove financially beneficial to both of them.

Guy knew little of Simon, who had come to Hamilton Corners about six months before this story opens. He had met him in the billiard room, where several youths of the town, who might better have been at something else, frequently gathered. Simon never appeared to work, but generally had plenty of money.

He dressed flashily, and his conversation was filled with allusions to this or that "sport." Guy, who aspired to be thought a gilded youth of the city, rather than a plain country lad, with a father moderately well off, at once made fast friends with Simon.

Because of the business relations of Dick's and Guy's fathers, the two lads had been more or less friendly for several years, and, when Guy took up with Simon, Dick did not hesitate to admit him to his house, where the boys frequently assembled to play billiards or other games, or practice in the fine gymnasium Mr. Hamilton had provided for his son.

Thus, though Dick was aware of the rather sporty character of Guy and Simon, he was frank and pleasant with them, for he was a youth of rather free and easy ways, in spite of his wealth.

Dick would have been glad to take all his boy friends of Hamilton Corners with him to New York, but the capacity of the automobile was limited to seven; so, besides Dick, Simon and Guy, there went along "Bricktop," Frank Bender and Walter Mead.

Early on the appointed morning the big touring car, in charge of a skillful driver, drew up in front of Dick's house, where the boys had assembled.

"Get in!" called Dick, from the window of his room. "I'll be right down as soon as I can get my valise shut. I've got to say good-bye to Grit. Poor fellow, he knows something's in the wind and he's trying to break his chain to come along. But I'm afraid something will happen to him in New York, so he's got to stay home."

"He thinks as much of that dog as if it was a brother," remarked Guy with something of a sneer, as the five youths entered the tonneau, for Dick had elected to ride with the driver.

"I don't blame him," said "Bricktop." "Grit's a dog worth having."

"I hope Dick brings plenty of money along with him," whispered Simon to Guy, as they followed Frank Bender into the machine.

"Why?" asked Guy, also in a whisper.

"Because I've got everything all planned for a neat trick. I guess he'll not bring back as much as he takes away. I heard from my friend in New York. He'll meet us at the hotel, and then—well, we'll see what will happen."

Dick came running down the steps of the mansion.

"Good-bye!" he called to his father. "Yes, I'll be careful—good-bye!"

There was a tooting of the automobile horn, a throbbing of the powerful engine, a grinding sound as the gears were thrown into place, and the boys were off on their trip to New York, Dick with his heart full of happiness and anticipation, while Simon and Guy were thinking over the plot they had made to get away from the millionaire's son a little of his wealth.

CHAPTER VII

A SHARPER FOILED

Through Hamilton Corners the big car shot, its progress watched by throngs who had heard of Dick's trip. His conduct was commented on in various ways.

"Good land!" exclaimed Hank Darby. "If I had the money that spendthrift will get rid of before he gets back here I could make my fortune. All I need is a little capital and I'd be rich inside of a week. I have a great scheme on."

"Ain't goin' t' buy any more soap, be ye, Hank?" asked Porter Heavydale, a little, thin, wisp of a man, who was fully as lazy as Hank, but who made no secret of it. "Guess you had some slip-up there."

"Oh, that—that was an accident, such as is liable to happen to any business man," and Hank carefully whittled a stick until there was nothing left of it.

"Wa'al, a fool an' his money is soon parted, the proverb says," commented Porter. "Give Dick rope enough an' he'll come t' th' end of it sooner or later."

"Dick's no fool," retorted Hank. "But I do hate to see him spend money."

"Hasn't he a right to it, father?" asked Henry, always ready to come to Dick's defense. "It's his, and I'm sure he has been kind enough to me. Why, he loaned me fifty dollars the other day."

"He did! Land sakes, where is it now, Henry? If I knowed that I could have made a deal with it. Git it for me right away."

"I can't," replied Henry. "I bought some old iron with it and I'm waiting for a raise in the market. Besides, it's only a loan."

"He'll never miss it," said Mr. Darby. "Good land! I wished I a-knowed you had it! I could 'a' bought some oil well stock. It's awful cheap now."

"Yes, an' it would be a heap sight cheaper after you'd bought it," put in Porter with a laugh.

New York was reached by those in the touring car at nightfall, and Dick registered himself and his friends at one of the finest hotels, the manager of which his father knew. The boys had adjoining rooms in the best part of the big building, and

"Bricktop," Frank and Walter were so excited over the beautifully fitted-up apartments that they could do nothing but stare about.

"Oh, they're not so bad," remarked Simon, in a patronizing tone when appealed to by "Bricktop," who demanded to know if this wasn't "the best ever." Simon had never been in such a fine hotel, but he wanted to pretend he was used to the luxuries. Guy followed his crony's example and affected to sneer at the accommodations.

"My father and I generally put up at one of the better hotels," he said affectedly. "But, of course, this is all right for roughing it."

"Roughing it!" exclaimed Walter. "Come off! Why, it's good enough for a king here."

"Oh, well, wait until you've been about a bit," answered Simon languidly.

After supper Dick took his friends to a theatre, where a war-time play was in progress, and even Simon and Guy enthused over the stirring scenes.

The next day was spent in visiting Central Park, the big zoo at Bronx Park, and the Museums of Art and Natural History.

Simon acted as escort, for he was fairly well acquainted with objects of interest in New York, and Dick good-naturedly let him pilot the boys about as though Simon was paying for it all instead of the millionaire's son footing the bills.

It was not long before a keen reporter had learned of the presence in New York of the wealthy youth of whom the papers had recently contained so much, and there appeared several items telling of the trip. There were a number of incorrect stories in print, and Dick was credited with having expended nearly ten thousand dollars on his simple little pleasure jaunt.

The result of this was that Dick was visited by a number of cranks, or, rather, they came to the hotel; but the wise manager, who had been telephoned to by Mr. Hamilton, had an eye to the wealthy youth's comfort, and few of the bothersome ones got beyond the lobby.

"I say," spoke Guy to Simon, on the afternoon of the third day in New York, when Dick was in the far end of the room, writing a letter home, "when are you going to pull off that trick, Simon?"

"This evening," was the cautious answer. "I've seen Colonel Dendon, and he's coming here to-night. I'm going to introduce him to Dick. The colonel says he'll whack up with me whatever he gets out of him, and I'll see that you get your share."

"But, say," went on Guy. "This is no gold-brick swindle, is it? I wouldn't do anything wrong—or—er—criminal—you know. Is it all right?"

"Of course it is!" exclaimed Simon, with a show of indignation. "Do you think I'd do anything that wasn't right, or for which I could be—er—get into trouble?"

"I didn't know," ventured Guy.

"Of course I wouldn't," continued Simon, with a great show of indignation that any one should suspect him. "This thing is perfectly legitimate. I know a certain party here—Colonel Dendon by name—who has all kinds of stocks and bonds for sale. Some are better than others. On some he can make a large profit. They may not be quite as good as those some other men have, but that's not the fault of Colonel Dendon, or you or me. It's the fault of the market.

"He's often said to me that if I could introduce him to somebody with money—somebody who'd buy some of his stocks—he'd give me twenty-five per cent. of what he made. It's a regular business deal. It's done every day. Colonel Dendon is a sort of a promotor. I'm only helping him. It's perfectly honest—that is, as honest—well, it's as honest as lots of things I know about. I wouldn't get you into any trouble, Guy."

"I hope not," answered the weak youth, who believed nearly all that Simon told him. "But if these stocks are good ones won't Dick make money on them? And if he does how is the colonel going to make any?"

"I didn't say for sure that the stocks were good," replied Simon. "They may be good for all I know. Maybe Dick will have to hold them for some time before he can realize on them. I don't bother with all those details. The colonel has stocks to sell—all kinds—I simply introduce Dick to him and he does the rest, and pays me and you for our trouble."

"Then I guess it's all right," assented Guy, a little doubtfully.

"Of course it is," declared Simon very positively.

That evening, as Dick and his friends sat in the private parlor of their suite of rooms, there was a knock at the door. Simon, being nearest it, answered, and, as soon as he had opened the portal, he exclaimed:

"Why, Colonel Dendon. Come right in. Richard, let me introduce you to Colonel Dendon, an old friend of mine," Simon added with a grand air. "Come right in, Colonel, I'm sure we're glad to see you," and Simon winked at the man who entered. The colonel was not at all war-like looking. He had shifty eyes, and a nervous manner. His white hair would seem to have indicated that he was elderly, but his white beard, which was stained by tobacco juice, did not tend to gain for him that respect for which silver locks generally call.

"I'll come in just for a minute—can't stay long—very busy," said the colonel jerkily, as he gave Dick a rather limp and flabby hand.

"I suppose you have some big deal on that won't keep," put in Guy, who was playing his part in the plot.

"That's it. Yes, I've got an appointment with some bank directors for seven o'clock, and one with the president of Pennsylvania Railroad at eight. A big bond sale involved. I heard you were in town, Simon, and I thought I'd look you up."

"Glad you did. But, by the way, I don't suppose you have anything in the line of investment that you would care to recommend to my friend, Mr. Hamilton, here? You've heard about him, I think." "Is this the young man who has so much money?" asked the colonel, with a start of seeming surprise.

"Well, I don't know that it's such an awful pile," said Dick with a laugh, for he disliked having his wealth talked about by strangers.

"I've read lots about you," went on Colonel Dendon. "No, I'm afraid I haven't anything that you would care for. I only deal in big sums."

"Well, Dick can command large sums," put in Guy, with an uneasy laugh.

"I don't suppose you would care to take a hundred thousand dollars worth of mining securities of a gilt-edge kind?" asked the colonel, looking at Dick.

"No, I'm hardly up to that yet. I intend to do some investing sooner or later; but I'm going to begin small. A hundred thousand is a little too large for me just yet."

"I was afraid so," replied Colonel Dendon, with a queer smile. "Well, I must be going. I'm a very busy man."

He turned as if about to leave the room, and then he suddenly seemed to remember something.

"Now I think of it, I have a few securities that I might let your friend have as a favor to you," he said, addressing Simon. "They are mining stocks. I took them from a man who failed, and I know they are valuable. They are worth to-day half as much again as I paid for them. But, as a favor to Mr. Hamilton, I'd let him have them at a small advance over what I paid. I have to do business on business principles," he added, with an air meant to be very important.

"Here's your chance, Dick," whispered Guy. "This man is a big stock operator. You can almost double your money and make up all you spent on this trip."

Dick was doing some rapid thinking. The loss of the money he had invested in the land was something of a disappointment to him. Then, too, he felt under the necessity of making some kind of a paying investment. He had a vision of Uncle Ezra and the house at Dankville, and the memory of that gloomy place made him wish to comply as soon as possible with the terms of his mother's will.

"I don't mind investing some money, say five hundred or a thousand dollars, in good mining stocks—if you are sure they are good," he said, turning to Colonel Dendon.

"Good! My dear young man, do you wish to insult me? As if I would deal in stocks that were anything but the best. I shall leave at once!" and, puffing up like an angry toad, the colonel again turned as if to go.

"Wait!" exclaimed Simon. "I'm sure my friend Dick didn't mean anything, Colonel. You see, he has never bought mining stocks before, and he doesn't know much about them."

"I know enough to want to be sure they are good!" replied Dick sharply, for he rather resented Simon's tone. "I'm not going to be swindled."

"Of course not," said the colonel, in less aggrieved tones. "I was a little too hasty. But I can assure you, Mr. Hamilton, that these securities are the very best of their kind. They are gilt-edged."

As he spoke he drew from his pocket a bundle of certificates which, as far as appearances went, were "gilt-edged," for there was a broad band of gilt all around them.

"I can let you have these for eight hundred dollars," he said; "and they will be worth a thousand inside of a month. I would keep them myself only I have bigger schemes on hand. I will let you have them as a special favor, Mr. Hamilton."

Dick examined the certificates. They certainly looked just like those he had often seen in his father's bank. They bore a number of flourishing signatures and a printed notice to the effect that they were listed on the New York Stock Exchange. They called for a number of shares of stock in a Pennsylvania oil well concern.

Dick felt impelled to take them. It seemed all right, even if he did have some lingering suspicion regarding the colonel. Still, appearances might be against him, and certainly Simon seemed to know the man.

Dick saw a vision of his investment turning out well, so he would have no further worry about fulfilling the conditions of the will. Once they were met he could enjoy his new wealth.

"I think I'll take these," he said, reaching for his pocket-book, where he carried several hundred dollars, though he had left some of his money in the hotel safe. "I will give you part cash and a check."

"It will be a fine investment," said Colonel Dendon; but he did not say for whom. "I can assure you, Mr. Hamilton, that I never sold such gilt-edged securities before. I am glad——"

At that instant the door of Dick's apartments opened, and a quietly-dressed man entered. He looked at the group of boys, noted the bundle of stock certificates, and then his glance rested on Colonel Dendon.

"I must ask you to leave this hotel at once," he said sharply, to the white-haired man. "If you don't go I shall be under the necessity of putting you under arrest."

CHAPTER VIII

DICK AND THE REPORTER

For a few moments after the surprising announcement, no one spoke. The boys and Colonel Dendon stared at the newcomer. The colonel was the first to recover himself.

"What is the meaning of this unwarranted intrusion?" he demanded, in pompous tones. "These young gentlemen and myself were discussing some financial matters when you interrupt us. You have doubtless made a mistake, and I will overlook it this time. Withdraw at once, sir, or I shall have to call the servants and have you thrown out of these private apartments, sir!"

"Better go easy," suggested the quiet-looking man, with just the suggestion of a smile. "If there's any throwing out to be done I reckon I'll take a hand in it."

"What do you mean, sir? Leave the room at once!" exclaimed the colonel, getting red in the face.

"I mean just this, William Jackson, *alias* Colonel Dendon, *alias* Bond Broker Bill!" said the man sharply, "that you must leave this hotel at once or I shall arrest you. You can't conduct any of your swindling games here—trying to sell fake stocks and bonds. I saw you come in, and learned that you were calling on this young man," and he nodded to Dick, who was much surprised at the proceeding. "I got up here in time to warn him, I see. I hope you haven't given him any money?" he asked of the millionaire's son.

"I—I was just going to—for some bonds he had."

"Lucky I came in," was the man's reply. "Now beat it, Bill," and he waved his hand toward the door. "Take your trash with you," he added, sweeping the bonds from the table.

Dick and the other boys, with the possible exception of Simon, expected to see the colonel defend himself and indignantly reply to the stranger. Instead he hurriedly gathered up his papers and fairly raced from the room.

"Is he—is he a swindler?" asked Dick, faintly.

"One of the slickest in New York," was the answer. "His game is to sell fake bonds in companies that never existed, though some of them are legally organized. Once in a while, just to fool the police, he deals in regular stocks, but the kind he usually sells are fake ones. I'm the hotel detective," the man went on. "We have to be always on the lookout for such chaps as he is, especially when we have young millionaires stopping at the house," and he smiled at Dick.

"I'm much obliged to you," answered Dick heartily. "You've saved me a considerable sum."

"That's what I'm here for," returned the detective cheerfully. "Don't go buying any gold bricks, now," and, with a nod at the boys, he was gone.

"Well, wouldn't that rattle your teeth!" exclaimed "Bricktop." "I've read about those confidence men and green-goods swindlers, but I never saw one before."

"Me, either," remarked Frank Bender. "Say, this will be something to tell the folks back home," and, in the excitement of his spirits he tried to stand on his head in a washbowl on the stand. It was full of water, and his acrobatic feat was brought to an abrupt end as he lifted his head, dripping wet.

"That's a new way to do it!" exclaimed Walter Mead, with a laugh.

"Ugh! Burrrr! Wow! Whew! Give me a towel, quick!" yelled Frank. "The water had soap in it, and it's got in my eyes!"

He groped around with outstretched hands, seeking a towel, which, after he was able to stop laughing, Dick handed him.

"Did you know that Colonel Dendon was a swindler?" asked Walter of Simon, when the excitement had somewhat subsided.

"Me? No, of course not!" exclaimed Simon hastily. "All I knew was that he sold bonds, and I thought it would be a good chance for Dick to make money. He said he wanted to learn business and make money. I—I was as much surprised as any of you," concluded Simon, with an injured air. "I hope you don't think, Dick, that I would have had anything to do with that man if I had known what he was?"

"I'm not blaming you any," replied Dick. "Mistakes will happen in the best of regulated financial affairs. Glad that detective happened to come in when he did or I might have been badly stung."

It was now too late to go out to any amusement and the boys, after discussing the recent happenings, went to bed, planning to visit many points of interest the next day.

"Well, your scheme didn't work out, did it?" said Guy to Simon, as they went to their rooms.

"Not exactly," was the answer. "But I give you my word I didn't know the colonel was such a swindler as that. Never mind, though, I'll make money out of Dick—somehow."

Dick and his chums had scarcely finished their breakfast the next morning, and were preparing to go out, when the bell boy brought up a card reading:

LAWRENCE DEXTER

New York Leader

"Who is it?" asked "Bricktop," "another man to sell bonds?"

Dick handed over the card.

"*New York Leader*, eh? I wonder what he leads, a band or some political party?"

"That's a reporter," said Walter. "Going to let him in, Dick?"

"Yes, I guess so. I'm tired of having stuff in the papers about me; but these reporters have to get the stories they're sent after, and it's no use making it any harder for them than they have it. Tell him to come up," he said to the waiting bell boy.

A tall, good-looking youth, with a pleasant, manly air, entered the room.

To those who have read some of my other books he will not be a stranger, for he was none other than Larry Dexter, whose various adventures I have described in "The Great Newspaper Series," starting with "From Office Boy to Reporter."

"Which one is the millionaire's son, with money to burn?" Larry asked, with a laugh that showed in his eyes. He was a little older than Dick.

"I suppose I am," answered the wealthy youth.

"I'm from the *Leader*," said Larry Dexter. "I've been sent to get your impressions of New York, and to ask whether you find it a good place to spend money. Do you mind talking for publication?"

There was such a winning way about this reporter, so different from that noticeable in many of the newspaper men Dick had been inflicted with, that the millionaire's son liked him at once. Larry did not take it for granted that Dick must submit to the questions, but, in a gentlemanly way, asked for permission to "write him up."

"I don't know that I can tell you anything that will be of interest to the paper," said Dick, "but I'll do my best."

"That's a relief," returned Larry. "I just came from a crusty old man—a professor who has discovered a new way of making milk keep—and he was so grouchy I couldn't get a word out of him. It's a big change to find somebody who will talk."

"Please don't make up a lot of silly, sensational stuff?" pleaded Dick. "I'm tired of all that. I'm no different from other fellows."

"Oh, yes, you are!" interrupted Larry with a laugh. "You have millions of money, and you'll find that makes all the difference in the world. It will gain you friends, position—in fact, almost anything. At least so they tell me," he added with another smile. "I never had a million myself. But now let's get down to business. What do you think of New York? Can you spend money here as fast as you want to?"

"He came pretty near spending it faster than he wanted to last night," put in "Bricktop."

"How was that?" asked Larry quickly, feeling that there was "in the air," so to speak, a story out of the usual run.

Thereupon Dick told about the attempted bond swindle.

"Say, this is great!" exclaimed Larry. "This is the best yet! This beats having you talk about New York. Do me a favor, will you?"

"What is it?" inquired Dick. "If it's to buy some gilt-edged bonds, I'm afraid I'll have to decline."

"No, it's only this. Don't say anything about this bond business to any other reporters."

"I'm not likely to, unless they ask me to," replied Dick. "But why?"

"Because I want to get a beat out of it."

"A beat?" inquired "Bricktop," while the other boys looked puzzled.

"Yes. An exclusive story. I don't want the reporters for any other papers to get hold of it. If I have it all alone in the *Leader* it will be a feather in my cap. News that no other paper has is the very best kind."?

"Gilt-edged, I suppose," put in Dick.

"That's it," replied Larry quickly. "Now don't tell any other reporters, will you?"

"Well, if they come here and ask about it, I can't say it wasn't so."

"No, I suppose not," assented Larry. "But, I tell you what you can do."

"What?"

"Go for a walk, and don't come back to the hotel until after my paper is out with the story. We publish in the afternoon and go to press about noon for the first edition. Would it be asking too much of you to do that?"

"No, for we were going out anyhow."

"Then come with me," suggested Larry. "I'll take you to the *Leader* office and have a man show you how we make a newspaper. I guess no other reporters will come in there to get the story out of you," and he laughed in delight at the "beat" he had secured.

Dick and his friends were only too glad to get a chance to see a big paper printed, and soon they were on their way to the *Leader* office, escorted by Larry.

"If any other reporters see me they'll think I'm taking some young men's club on a tour of the city," the young journalist remarked, as the little throng walked along. "Well, if they do, it will be a good way to throw them off the scent."

Larry reported to his city editor about having most unexpectedly come across a "big" story in connection with the young millionaire, and was told to "let it run for all it's worth."

"I'll see to it that the modern Crœsus and his friends are entertained," said Mr. Newton, another reporter, who was told by Mr. Emberg, the city editor, to show Dick and his chums around the newspaper plant.

It was getting close to edition time, and they noticed, with much amazement, how the reporters came hurrying in with the news they had gathered; how they sat down at typewriters and rattled it off; how it was corrected and edited; sent to the composing room in pneumatic tubes; set up on type-setting machines that seemed almost human; the type put into "forms" or strong steel frames; how a soft sheet of wet paper was pressed on the type and baked by steam until it took every impression and was the exact counterpart of a printed page.

The boys watched and saw that these baked sheets of paper, called "matrices," were sent to the stereotyping room, where, bent into a half-circle in a machine, they were filled with hot melted lead, which, hardening, took every impression of the cardboard.

Then the curved metal plates, each one representing a page of the paper, were clamped on a big press, that worked with a noise like thunder, and, in an instant, it seemed, white paper from a big roll, which was fed it at one end, came out printed, pasted, and folded newspapers at the other end of the machine.

A grimy boy gathered up an armful of them, as they kept piling up at the foot of a chute, which extended somewhere up inside the press. Mr. Newton, who had escorted Dick and his friends about, took up one of the journals.

"There you are!" he shouted, above the rumble and roar of the press, as he handed Dick a paper.

The wealthy youth unfolded it. On the front page was the story of himself and "Colonel Dendon." It was under a "scare" head, which announced:

ATTEMPTED SWINDLE OF YOUNG MILLIONAIRE!

SHARPER TRIES TO SELL TO DICK HAMILTON, WHO RECENTLY INHERITED VAST WEALTH, WORTHLESS BONDS!

DETECTIVE ACTS IN TIME

"Humph!" murmured Dick, when he saw what a big story Larry had made of it. "If my father saw this he'd be worried."

"You're getting more famous than ever!" exclaimed Walter Mead.

"Looks so," admitted the young millionaire. "Well, I'm glad Larry got his beat, anyhow."

And it was a beat, for, when Dick got back to the hotel, the manager told him half the newspapers in New York had been calling him up to ask about the story.

CHAPTER IX

A CIRCUS COMES TO TOWN

Dick and his friends went home in the big automobile a few days later, having crowded into their stay as much sight-seeing as was possible. Dick had just finished telling his father, the evening of his arrival, of his various adventures, including the one with the swindler, when the servant announced:

"Some one to see you, Master Dick."

"Who is it?"

"Henry Darby."

"Ah, there's a young man who will make his mark some day!" exclaimed Mr. Hamilton. "If his father was only like him Henry would have more chances."

"That's right," admitted Dick. "I wonder what he wants?"

"Well, I'll leave you together," said Dick's father, as he left the library, and a little later Henry was ushered in by the servant.

"Hello, Henry!" exclaimed Dick.

"Same to you and more of it," was Henry's greeting. "I've come to see if you don't want a particularly fine line of gold bricks," he went on with a laugh, for he had read in the papers of the attempted bond swindle.

"You'll have to see my secretary," spoke Dick, joining in the spirit of the talk. "He buys all my gold bricks. But, to change the subject, how's the old iron business?"

"Pretty good. In fact, I came to see you about it, if you're not too busy," and Henry tried to look as though he had come to discuss the investment of millions.

"No, I guess I can spare you a few minutes. What is it?"

"I came to take up my note and pay it off," went on the young iron merchant, drawing a roll of much-crumpled bills from his pocket. "Want to save interest, you know. I managed to sell that iron I bought, and I made a profit on it. So I'll pay that fifty-dollar note now."

"Well, you certainly know how to make money," spoke Dick admiringly. "I'll have to take lessons from you. But say, Henry, I'm in no hurry for that money. If you can use it, why, just keep it."

"No—no," went on Henry, with rather a sorrowful air, Dick thought. "I'd better pay you while I have it. I might not be able to get it together again. You take it," and he shoved the bills over toward Dick with an air of desperation.

"But, I don't need it," persisted Dick. "You might just as well keep it a while, Henry."

"Do you mean that?" asked Henry earnestly.

"Sure."

"Then I will," and Henry appeared much relieved.

"In fact, if you want more I'll lend it to you," continued the millionaire's son.

"Are you in earnest?"

"Of course I am. Why?"

"Well, to tell you the truth I hated to pay back that fifty dollars. I mean I still had a use for it. In fact, if I had a little more I could branch out—I'm a sort of a little tree now—like one of those saplings they set out. I need branches."

"Tell me about it," suggested Dick.

"Well, if I had two hundred dollars more I could buy out the business of Moses Cohen, who deals in old metal. He's getting too feeble to carry it on, and I heard it was for sale. I made some inquiries and I found I can get it for about five hundred dollars."

"But you said two hundred and fifty was all you needed."

"So it is. I'm only going to pay half cash, and give a mortgage for the balance. That's the safest way. So I was in hopes you wouldn't take that fifty. I might induce him to take this on account and wait a while for the two hundred."

"He needn't wait at all," interrupted Dick. "I'll let you have two hundred more, with pleasure," and he drew out his check book with a little flourish.

"I can't give you any security but my note," said Henry. "Even that wouldn't be good in law, as I am not of age. But it shows I mean to pay you back."

"Of course it does."

"I'll get my father to give you his, also," went on the young lad of business. "Though I guess it isn't worth much more than mine," and he sighed a little, for Henry was aware of his father's failing.

"Yours is all I want," said Dick. "Tear up this old note and make out one for two hundred and fifty dollars. Then you can buy out Cohen's business."

Henry tore up the fifty-dollar promissory note Dick handed him and soon had made out another for the larger amount.

"There's the check," went on Dick, handing it over.

"I'll get dad to draw up some kind of a paper giving you a share in the business," continued Henry. "He heard about me going to buy out old Cohen, and he wants me to incorporate and make him one of the officers. I guess that's what he's best fitted for," and once more Henry smiled rather sadly.

"Well, I wish you good luck," returned Dick as he shook hands with Henry. "I'm going to put through some business deals myself soon, as for certain reasons, I've got to make a good investment," and he thought of his failure in the land scheme, while a vision of his Uncle Ezra came to him like the memory of a bad dream.

It was several days after this that Dick met Frank Bender on the street. Frank was attired in his "Sunday clothes" and seemed in a hurry.

"Where you going?" asked Dick.

"Circus."

"Where is it?"

"Over to Parkertown. They have some good acrobats in it, and I want to get a few points."

"I wonder why a circus never comes here," mused Dick, half to himself. "It's quite a trip to Parkertown."

"This place is too small," replied Frank.

"They have to have a big crowd to make it pay. A circus will never come here."

"No, I s'pose not," answered Dick. "Well, I wish I was going, but I've got to go down to dad's bank. I've got a little business on hand."

"So long," called Frank. "I must hurry to catch the train."

"I wish they'd have a circus here some time," continued Dick, as he walked along. "Hamilton Corners is too quiet. It needs stirring up."

Just then he caught sight of a curious procession. It was composed of a number of boys and girls, mostly little tots, walking along the street, two by two, led by three matronly ladies.

"The orphan asylum out for an airing," commented Dick. "Poor little kids! Poor little kids!"

There was a county orphan asylum in Hamilton Corners, and it was usually well filled with small unfortunates. Twice a week they were taken for a walk by some of the matrons in charge.

"Poor little kids!" repeated Dick. "I'll bet they never saw a circus in their lives. And they're not likely to. A circus will never come here. The place is too small. No, they'll never see a circus—unless——"

He came to a sudden stop in his musings. Then a light broke over his face.

"By Jimminy Crickets! I'll do it!" he exclaimed, so loudly that several persons in the street turned to look at him. "I'll do it! That's what I will!"

He looked at his watch.

"I've just got time to catch the train to Parkertown if I hustle," he added as he set off on a run.

CHAPTER X

DICK INVESTS IN HAPPINESS

Dick managed to swing aboard the last car as the train for Parkertown was pulling out of the station at Hamilton Corners. There was quite a crowd on it, as many were going to the circus.

"Hello!" exclaimed Frank Bender, as he caught sight of Dick walking up the aisle of the car in which he was. "I thought you weren't going."

"I wasn't, but I changed my mind. This is a free country."

"Of course," assented Frank, with a laugh. "We'll go together and have some fun."

"Oh, I'm going on business."

"That's too bad."

"Well, it's business connected with fun," explained Dick. "Maybe I'll have a chance to see the show with you later."

"See the show! Why, that's the main object of going to Parkertown," responded Frank. "I wouldn't miss it for anything. They've got a fellow in it, according to the pictures, who can stand on his head, hold a man in each hand, balance two others on his legs, hold one by a strap in his mouth—and all the while he's on a trapeze at the top of the tent. It's great!"

"Well, maybe he can give you a few pointers," said Dick.

It was about an hour's run to Parkertown, and when the train reached the circus grounds there was a general rush to the big tents. It lacked about an hour to noon, and though the show had not opened yet there was much of interest to see. Dick and Frank watched the men putting finishing touches to the immense canvas shelters, while others were feeding the animals, getting the big gilded wagons into place, and arranging the sideshows.

In one tent hundreds of the performers and helpers were at dinner, while a curious crowd looked on under the raised flaps. The two boys, in company with scores of others, watched the cooks of the circus at work over the portable ranges and soup kettles, where it seemed as though enough food for an army was being prepared.

"Say, it's great, isn't it!" exclaimed Frank. "I can hardly wait until it's time to begin. Let's go get a hot frankfurter sausage somewhere."

"I'm afraid I've got to leave you," replied Dick. "I have some business on hand. I'll see you later. Maybe in the main tent."

"All right," assented Frank, a little disappointed, but he soon forgot about that in watching the many scenes of interest.

"Where can I find the manager?" asked Dick, of a man who wore a uniform and seemed to be some one in authority.

"In the ticket wagon," was the reply. "But you needn't think you can deadhead in. The free list is suspended."

"I've no intention of asking for a pass," replied Dick, with a smile. "Is the manager in?" he asked, a moment later, of the man who looked out of the high ticket wagon.

"I guess so. What do you want?"

"I want to see him in regard to the next town where he is to play."

"Who is it?" inquired a voice from within the vehicle.

"Some lad from our next town. Maybe the mayor's sent to say he's going to raise the license fee. I never see such a hold-up game as these country mayors try to pull off," and the ticket seller looked disgusted.

"No, I'm not from the mayor," said Dick. "I want to see the manager on my own account."

At this another man joined the one at the ticket window. He was large and fat, and wore a red necktie, in which sparkled a pin with a large stone. He had on a tall hat and a frock coat.

"Come around to the side door," he said, in no very gracious tones, and Dick noticed that a pair of steps at the side gave access to the wagon. He was soon inside the place, which was fittedup like a small office, with desks, and even a typewriter, at which a young man was busy pounding the keys.

"What is it?" asked the manager, abruptly.

"I've come to see if you won't give a show in Hamilton Corners," began Dick. "I think the town would like to see it."

"Maybe the town would, but I wouldn't," replied the manager quickly. "I'm not in business for my health. I want to make a little money, and Hamilton Corners is too small. We couldn't clear expenses."

"How much do you have to clear to make it worth your while to show in a town?" asked Dick.

"Well, a thousand dollars is fair business."

"If you were sure of a thousand dollars clear, would you come to Hamilton Corners?"

"Yes, or any place else within traveling distance. But what are you? A newspaper reporter? If you are, you want to see our press agent. He's in that tent over there."

"No, I want to do business with you," rejoined Dick, with a smile. "I live in Hamilton Corners. I'd like to see a circus there. In fact, I'm willing to pay for having one come there. I have a certain reason for it. If I give you a thousand-dollar guarantee will you bring the show there?"

"Yes, of course."

The manager seemed a little dazed. Dick drew out a thin red book.

"I'll give you the guarantee now," he said. "Can you come to-morrow?" and he began to use his fountain pen. "Whom shall I make it out to?" and he looked at the manager.

"Say," suddenly whispered the manager to the ticket seller. "Is the marshall out there? He is? All right. Call him here." Then in soothing tones he spoke to Dick. "That's all right," he said. "Never mind the check. We'll come to Hamilton Corners, anyhow. Now don't get excited. Here, take a drink of water and you'll feel better. The sun is very hot to-day. In fact, it makes my head buzz. Just put that red book away. Red is very heating, you know."

He paused, and looked rather helplessly about him. Then in a whisper he again asked the ticket seller:

"Is the marshall there? Tell him to come in before he gets violent."

The side door opened, and a town marshall, with a big nickel-plated star on his coat, entered the wagon.

"What's the matter?" asked Dick, somewhat surprised at the sudden turn of events.

"There! there!" spoke the manager, soothingly. "It's all right. Don't get excited. You're with friends."

"Don't you want this check?" asked Dick. "I'm in earnest. I want your circus to come to Hamilton Corners."

"Yes, yes, of course, my dear boy. We'll come. I'll let you ride on one of the elephants. You can feed the monkeys, and tickle the hippopotamus, if you like. Poor boy," in lower tones, "so young, too."

"Say," demanded Dick, standing up, "do you think I'm crazy?"

"There! there!" repeated the manager, in that soothing tone he had suddenly adopted. "Please don't get excited. It's the worst thing in the world for you."

Dick glanced up at the man in uniform. Then a smile came over his face that had assumed a rather angry look.

"Why, Marshall Hinckly!" he exclaimed. "How did you come to be here?"

"Dick Hamilton!" exclaimed the officer in surprise, "I didn't know you at first. You see the authorities in Parkertown, being a little short-handed, asked me to help out on circus day, and so I came over from Hamilton Corners. But what in the name of green turtles is the trouble here?"

"I don't know," replied the millionaire's son. "I merely offered to guarantee this manager a thousand dollars if he would bring his circus to Hamilton Corners, and he acts as though he thought I was crazy."

"And isn't he?" burst out the manager, less frightened, now that an officer of the law was present. "Isn't he, Mr. Policeman? The idea of a boy like him offering to make out a check for a thousand dollars to have a circus come to town! In the first place, I don't believe he has the money; and in the second, what does he want to hire a circus for? Say, honest, hasn't he got away from some asylum?"

"Dick Hamilton broke out of an asylum!" exclaimed the marshall. "Well, I rather guess not! As for him not having the money, you're wrong there. Why, that's Mortimer Hamilton's son," and he showed his pride at being acquainted with Dick.

"Mortimer Hamilton, president of the Hamilton National Bank?" asked the manager, incredulously.

"That's him," replied the marshall.

"Say!" exclaimed the manager rather faintly, sitting limply down in a chair. "Give me a glass of water, will you, please. Mortimer Hamilton, the multi-millionaire! And I thought his son didn't have a thousand dollars! Excuse me, Mr. Hamilton," he said, heartily, as he held out his hand to Dick. "I beg your pardon."

"That's all right," replied Dick, with a smile. "Whom shall I make the check out to?"

"Me," replied the manager. "Wellington Dappleton. But say," he added, "would you mind telling me what you want of the circus?"

"I'll tell you," answered Dick, with something of a serious air. "When I was out walking this morning I saw a procession from the orphan asylum. I heard about the circus being over here, and I knew those poor youngsters couldn't go. I made up my mind that if I could, I'd have the circus come to town and I'd take those kids free. It's the only chance they'll ever get, maybe, and I—well, I've got plenty of money. I can just as well spend some of it this way as in having a good time myself. When can you come?"

"We'll be there to-morrow and play the afternoon and evening," said the manager. "And I'll tell you what I'll do. You needn't make out that check now. We'll wait until after the last performance, and all I'll ask you to do will be to make good whatever I'm short of a thousand-dollar profit. Maybe we can get enough admissions in the town to make up part of the sum. I'll not see a lad do the only good turn in these parts. I'll meet you half way, and there's my hand on it," and once more he gripped Dick's fingers in a hold that made them tingle.

"But the orphans come in free," insisted Dick.

"The orphans come in free," repeated the manager, "and any other boys or girls you like. We'll only charge the grown folks."

So it was arranged. Dick and the manager had a long talk, so long that Dick had time only to see the closing acts in the big tent.

"Well, you missed it," said Frank, as he met Dick on his way out. "You should have seen that fellow hold all those others. It was great! I'm going to join a circus."

"Better wait," advised Dick, with a smile. "Have a talk with that acrobat. The show is coming to Hamilton Corners to-morrow, and you can ask him how he likes the life."

"The show coming to Hamilton Corners?"

"Yes," and then Dick told of the arrangements.

Hamilton Corners hardly knew itself when it awoke the next morning. The town was gay with many colored posters, showing fierce animals wandering together over vast treeless plains, and many-hued lithographs of men risking their lives on the high trapeze. Before the boys had fairly gotten the idea into their heads that the circus was coming the cavalcade of wagons began arriving. Dick had seen the town authorities and secured the necessary permits. Then Hamilton Corners really woke up as the news became known that Dick was responsible for the whole affair.

"Say, he spends money like water," observed Simon to Guy. "I wish I had some of what he's throwing away."

"I suppose you'd buy oil stock with it," observed Guy, with a peculiar smile. Simon did not answer.

The orphans at the asylum—hundreds of them—could hardly believe the joyous news when, after Dick had told those in charge, it was announced to them by the matrons. Some of the poor little tots cried in very happiness. One little boy, who remembered once seeing some of the gay lithographs of a circus, was discovered running around in a circle.

"What are you doing?" asked a matron.

"Playing I'm a circus horse," was the answer. "I'se got to do suffin to make de time pass. I'm so happy!"

Long before the time set for the performance, crowds of boys and girls were headed for the big tents. Dick had generously arranged so that no boy or girl need pay, and hundreds of those in Hamilton Corners, as well as those in the surrounding suburbs, besides the orphans, saw the show free.

Dick wanted to go off with some of his chums and view the performance, but the head matron of the asylum asked him to sit with her in the midst of her little charges.

"They want to see you," she explained. "They think you own the circus, and that you are the most wonderful person in the world."

"Oh, pshaw! It isn't anything at all," declared Dick, with a blush. "I just happened to think of it when I saw the little children out walking and saw how sad some of 'em looked. Besides, it's time we had a circus in Hamilton Corners."

The antics of the clowns, the "hair-raising, death-defying evolutions in mid-air," as the programme called them, the performing horses and elephants, the pony races, the chariot contests, the trick dogs, pigs, monkeys, and other animals, the glittering pageant, the music and excitement—all this was as a happy dream to the orphans. They sat in ecstasy, now and then some of them looking at Dick, who sat in their midst, as though, like some good fairy, they feared he might disappear any minute.

"Well," remarked the manager to Dick in the library of the Hamilton mansion, when the show was over. "You had your circus all right. I guess about four hundred dollars will square us. There were quite a few paid admissions."

"There's your check," answered Dick, passing over a slip of paper, and the manager took his departure.

That night, as the rumble of circus wagons leaving the town came faintly to the ears of Dick and his father, as they sat in the library, Mr. Hamilton remarked:

"Well, did you get your money's worth, Dick?"

"I certainly did, dad. The look on the faces of those orphans was worth twice as much as I spent."

"Still, you might have invested four hundred dollars in some business and gotten large returns from it."

"I invested it in happiness, dad," was Dick's answer.

And then Mr. Hamilton turned away, loving his son more than ever. But still he wondered if Dick would ever be able to fulfil the conditions of his mother's will.

CHAPTER XI

"Hank" Darby in Business

Hamilton Corners did not cease talking of the circus, and Dick's part in it, for several weeks. Among the boys, Dick was more of a hero than ever and many were his champions. Only Simon and Guy sneered, but they took care to do it when no one else was present. The truth was, Simon hated to see Dick spend money unless he had a chance to get some of it, and, since the failure of the bond scheme, this did not seem very likely to happen.

For Mr. Hamilton had warned his son not to get too intimate with Simon. A youth, he said, who had as a friend a man of the character of Colonel Dendon was not a safe chum. Dick promised not to have too much to do with either Simon or Guy, but he was too independent a boy to cut them altogether.

"Are you going to be busy this afternoon, dad?" asked Dick of his father one morning. "Because if you're not, I'd like to come down to the bank and talk over a little business with you. I think it's about time I made some large investment in order to comply with mother's will, and I want to ask your advice."

"Come along," answered Mr. Hamilton, good-naturedly. "I will aid you all I can, but I'd rather you would learn to depend on yourself. Experience is the best teacher, but her lessons come a trifle high."

Several days previous to this Dick had been in correspondence with a New York firm, and he wanted some advice before he went any further into a certain scheme. Accordingly, at the time appointed, he went to his father's bank, carrying a lot of printed matter and some letters.

"Well, what is it?" asked Mr. Hamilton, when he and his son were seated in the private office.

"I was thinking of investing in this company, formed to supply a new kind of preserved milk," said Dick. "Some one has discovered a process by which milk can be made to keep a long time, and yet it tastes like fresh. They state that the milk problem, in big cities, is one that many have tried to solve. By their method any family can have fresh milk with little trouble, and it is almost as cheap as that which comes right from a cow. Of course, in a big city it's impossible to supply fresh milk to everyone.

"They are offering to sell some stock cheap, and it is guaranteed to double in value in six months. They are all ready to put the milk on the market. I was thinking of investing some money in this concern. What do you think of it?"

Mr. Hamilton looked over the mass of circulars, statements of the business that could be done in New York alone, to say nothing of the rest of the country, and glanced at the pictures of machines for making the milk so it would keep for a long time, without ice, even in the hottest weather.

"Well, Dick," he said slowly. "This company has some well-known men connected with it, and the scheme looks all right. That is as far as you can tell from this. If you want to invest some of your money in it I have no objections. How much did you figure on?"

"I thought about five thousand dollars."

Mr. Hamilton uttered a low whistle.

"I'd say two thousand," he remarked. "If you find it's good you can put the other three in later. Better go slow on a new thing. Of course, I don't know anything about it, and if it fails I don't want you to hold me responsible. I'm willing that you should try it—that's all."

"Then I'll send for two thousand dollars' worth of stock," decided Dick; and he made out a check, had it certified, and sent it to New York.

"Now that's done, and I'm in a fair way to make a large profit, I think I'll begin to look around for something else," he said. "It's a good thing to have several investments; isn't it, dad? I think I've heard you say not to have all your eggs in one basket."

"That's right," assented Mr. Hamilton. "Only you want to be sure you have good eggs, and not bad ones; also, that the baskets are strong enough to carry them."

At that moment there came a knock on the door of the private office, and when Mr. Hamilton had called out an invitation to enter, Archibald Spreckles McIverson, to give him his complete name, the messenger of the bank, announced:

"A gentleman to see you, Mr. Hamilton. I beg your pardon for interrupting you, but he says his business is very important and he will not detain you long. He also wishes to see Mr. Dick, and he has a young man with him."

"Show him in," said Mr. Hamilton. "Must be somebody with money," he added to his son as the messenger departed, "or McIverson would never be so puffed up. He loves to announce anyone whom he believes is wealthy, but I don't know of anyone, with any great amount of cash, who is coming to see me to-day."

"Mr. Henry Darby, senior and junior," announced Archibald Spreckles McIverson with a grand air, as he held the door of the private office open so that "Hank" Darby and Henry might enter. Then McIverson softly closed the portal.

"Ahem!" remarked Hank, almost as pompously as had the bank messenger. "Fine day, Mr. Hamilton."

Dick looked at Henry's father in amazement. The man was dressed in a new suit of black, and wore a silk hat. He had a necktie of vivid purple, and a red pink was in his buttonhole. He took off his tall hat and wiped his shining bald head with a big red silk handkerchief. No wonder he had impressed McIverson. Henry looked a little embarrassed, but Dick nodded at him in a friendly way, and made room for him on the sofa upon which he was sitting.

"I have called upon a little matter of business," said Mr. Darby, carefully depositing his hat on the carpet. "I and my son here," and he nodded in Henry's direction. "I may also add that your son is interested—er—to a considerable extent. In fact, I may say to an equal extent with ourselves."

"I wonder what's coming?" thought Mr. Hamilton, who had never seen Hank so well dressed, and who knew the man to be the laziest fellow in Hamilton Corners.

"Your son, Mr. Hamilton," went on Hank Darby, with a grand air that was strangely in contrast with his former attitude when one met him about town, "your son, I may state, has been the means of doing something which I long have desired to see done. He has enabled me and my son to start in business—a business that, while it is small, is capable of enormous possibilities—*enormous possibilities*," and Mr. Darby looked as if he would puff up like a balloon and float out of the window.

"In short," he went on, "he has loaned my son two hundred and fifty dollars, for which Henry has given his note. Of course, that is no legal security, and when I heard about it I at once set about putting the matter on a business basis."

"I don't understand," said Mr. Hamilton.

"Henry is in the old iron business, dad," explained Dick.

"Exactly," went on Mr. Darby. "The old metal business, to be more exact. I am also in it with him. Between us we have formed a company—a corporation to be more exact. I have called it The International and Consolidated Old Metal Corporation. We have a capital stock of one million dollars——"

"With two hundred and twenty-five paid in," interrupted Henry, with a smile. "Dad took twenty-five of your two hundred and fifty, Dick, to get himself some new clothes."

"Exactly," interrupted Mr. Darby. "As president of the International and Consolidated Old Metal Corporation I felt that it was due to the public to look the part. I don't mind old clothes myself, but the public is apt to judge a man by them. So I bought these. I think it will go a great way in impressing the public; do you not agree with me, sir?"

"Perfectly," answered Mr. Hamilton, trying not to smile.

"So you are president?" asked Dick.

"I am," replied Mr. Darby, with a grand air. "I am the president and you, sir, are the treasurer," and he bowed to Dick. "It is with your capital that we—my son and I— have been able to make this humble beginning. But all things must have a beginning. The possibilities are enormous, sir—*enormous!*" and once more Mr. Darby swelled up. "We are going to begin active operations at once, sir; in fact, my son has already begun them. We expect to do a large trade in metals of all description. I shall devote my time to the market abroad in a few weeks, as I shall have exhausted the possibilities on this side of the Atlantic. Then, sir, we shall be truly what the name indicated, *international!*"

"What do you do, Henry?" asked Dick.

"Me? Oh, I drive the wagon, collect the old iron and sell it again," said the lad, with just the suspicion of a smile, as he glanced in his father's direction. "I bought out old Moses Cohen, and he had a horse and wagon, which I took.

"At least, it's called a horse and wagon in the mortgage which I had to sign," went on Henry, "but sometimes I have my doubts about both," and he laughed a little. "However, it will do for a while—until I can make money enough to get a better rig."

"Yes, we are going a bit slow at first," put in Mr. Darby. "As soon as I get things in good shape I shall take a trip to England. I understand they use a great deal of iron there. Perhaps I shall buy up a large amount abroad and ship it here. I have a number of schemes on as soon as I get this one in such shape that Henry can run it—with the assistance of Mr. Dick, of course," he hastened to add.

"What we came here for to-day," said Henry, "was to give you these papers, Dick," and he handed over a large bundle.

"What are they?" asked Mr. Hamilton.

"The prospectus and incorporation papers of The International and Consolidated Old Metal Corporation," interrupted Mr. Darby. "I drew them up myself, and I know they are right. They show the interest you have in the concern," turning to Dick, "and your interests are fully looked after. I wish, also, to endorse the note my son gave you."

"It isn't necessary," declared Dick.

"Pardon me, young man, but it is," insisted Mr. Darby. "Business is business," he continued, with a grand air, and, when Dick produced the note, Mr. Darby, with a flourish, put his name on the back of it.

"It has doubled in value," he remarked, without the ghost of a smile. "Now, our matters being concluded, I will bid you good-afternoon," he said, and with a low bow to Mr. Hamilton and Dick, he backed out, attended by McIverson.

"If he'd let Henry alone the business might amount to something," commented Mr. Hamilton when the visitors had gone.

"Yes, the idea of his taking some of the money to buy a new suit," observed Dick. "Well, I guess Henry can manage it if he only has half a chance."

"I wouldn't give you much for that note," said Mr. Hamilton.

"You'll not discount it; eh, dad?"

"Not much! It's worse than ever since Hank put his signature on it. I guess your two hundred and fifty dollars are gone."

"Never mind, I helped Henry, anyhow. Maybe he'll pull through. He's a hard worker."

"Gentleman to see you, sir," interrupted McIverson, putting his head into the office. "Says he has an appointment with you."

"What is the name?" asked Mr. Hamilton.

"Mr. Franklin Vanderhoof," announced the messenger, with a rolling tone that denoted the person to be of apparent importance.

"Oh, yes. I'd forgotten. I'll see him at once. Dick, will you excuse me. I have some business to discuss with Mr. Vanderhoof."

As Dick bade his father good-bye and left the office he saw entering it a man, well dressed, and with a very black moustache. At the sight of the man's face Dick started.

"Where have I seen him before?" the youth asked himself. "There is something strange about that man. I wish I knew what his business was."

CHAPTER XII

GOLD MINE STOCK

Dick looked sharply at the stranger as he passed the man. Mr. Vanderhoof smiled, but when he did Dick thought the attempted pleasantry resembled the grin of a cat when it is about to pounce upon a helpless mouse. With a scarcely perceptible nod to Dick, Mr. Vanderhoof entered Mr. Hamilton's private office and closed the door.

"I've seen you before, I'm sure of it," mused Dick, as he left the bank. "I can't just think where, but there's something familiar about you. I don't like your looks, though I suppose you must be all right or dad wouldn't have much to do with you. I must ask him about you."

Dick found an opportunity a few evenings later. He saw his father looking over some papers in the library at home, and, going in, inquired if Mr. Hamilton was busy.

"Not very," replied the millionaire. "I'm just looking over some new stock I bought to-day. Dick, I'm part owner in a gold mine, in addition to my many other lines of industry," and he laughed pleasantly.

"A gold mine, dad?"

"Yes, a gold mine in—let's see where is it now—oh, in Yazoo City, Nevada. Of course, I don't own the whole mine, I've only bought some stock in it. There it is. I own a thousand shares in the Hop Toad Mine, and I hope they do as toads do, and 'jump' in value."

"A gold mine," repeated Dick. "That would suit me. Why didn't I think of it before."

"How do you mean, Dick?"

"I mean, why didn't I invest in something like that."

"Well, it's not too late, I suppose."

"Do you mean I can get some shares, dad?"

"I don't know that you can in the Hop Toad Mine, as I understand they're all sold out, but I guess Mr. Vanderhoof has shares in other mines just as good."

"Oh, is that what Mr. Vanderhoof is—a mining man?"

"Well, not exactly a mining man. He sells stock in mines. He's what they call a promoter. Why, do you know him?"

"No, but somehow his face seemed familiar. I was sure that day I saw him in the bank that I had met him somewhere else, but when I tried to think I couldn't recall anyone with such a black moustache as he has."

"It is black," admitted Mr. Hamilton.

"And when he smiles he looks like—a cat," went on Dick.

"I can't say that I fancy his looks," agreed the millionaire, with a chuckle. "But I don't do business on looks. I go by facts."

"Is this mining stock good?"

"I think so. I wrote to some men in Yazoo City and I made other investigations, so that I think it as safe an investment as any are in these days. Of course, nothing is a sure thing in this world, but I believe this Hop Toad Mine has one of the richest veins of ore of any mine in that vicinity."

"Then I'm going to invest some of my money in a gold mine," decided Dick. "Where can I find Mr. Vanderhoof?"

"He'll be at the bank to-morrow and you can see him there. Remember, you are doing this on your own responsibility, and if it turns out a failure you've got to chalk it up against yourself."

"All right, dad."

"It will be an experience for the boy, anyhow," murmured the millionaire, as his son left the room. "He's got to learn, the same as I did. I think between his mother's will, his Uncle Ezra, and what I can show him, we'll make a fine man of him in spite of his wealth, which is a mighty handicap—a mighty handicap," and shaking his head doubtfully Mr. Hamilton proceeded to look over some business papers, which task he was at when Dick went to bed.

Dick received a letter the next morning which rather disquieted him. It was from the firm of whom he had purchased his milk stock, and informed him that owing to certain contingencies in the market they were obliged to ask for an assessment on his stock.

"What's an assessment on stock, dad?" he asked of his father, when he had called at the bank and shown the letter to Mr. Hamilton.

"It means that the company needs more money to run the business, and that you, being part of the company, have to put up your share. Let's see, they want a hundred dollars from you. Well, I guess you'll have to pay it."

"But that's a queer way to do business," grumbled Dick. "I thought I was going to make money, and, instead, I have to pay out more."

"Oh, well, new concerns frequently have to call for an assessment, instead of paying dividends," consoled his father. "The stock may pay well yet. Milk is something every family has to have, you know, and they have to have it every day. The company may be all right when it gets well started. I wouldn't worry now. I've had to pay assessments on many a stock that afterward turned out well."

"I'm glad I thought of that gold mine stock," said Dick. "I guess that will be the best thing yet. When will Mr. Vanderhoof be here?"

"Almost any minute now. Ah, there he comes," and, as Mr. Hamilton spoke, the man with the very black moustache came down the corridor that led to the private office and walked through the open doorway.

"Ah, two captains of industry," he remarked, with a nod at Dick and his father. "The young and the—ah—er—I was about to say old—I will change it to junior and senior," with a bow to Mr. Hamilton.

"Dick thinks he'd like to buy some gold mine stock," said the millionaire. "I telephoned you about it, you recall, and explained my son's position."

"I understand," remarked Mr. Vanderhoof. "He wants to make a good paying investment."

"That's it," put in Dick, as he thought of his Uncle Ezra and what would happen if he did not comply with the terms of his mother's will.

"Well, I think I can find him some good stock," went on the promoter. "It won't be in the same mine you're in, Mr. Hamilton. That stock was too valuable to last long. But I have some nearly as good. It is in the same neighborhood. In fact, it is in the next mine to the Hop Toad—the Dolphin. We think it very good. You can make the same inquiries that you did in regard to the other stock. It will bear the closest investigation."

"We'll take it, subject to a report from Yazoo City," said Mr. Hamilton, with a look at Dick, who nodded an assent, for he knew very little about buying stock.

"Then I suppose you'll pay enough to bind the bargain?" asked Mr. Vanderhoof.

"Of course," replied Dick, producing his check book. "How much?"

"Five hundred dollars will do as a starter. But about how much stock would you want?"

"Oh, I guess two thousand dollars' worth will do," replied Dick, with a look at his father, who, by a nod of his head, assented.

Mr. Vanderhoof smiled, looking, Dick thought, more than ever like a cat about to pounce on a mouse, and when the check was made out the promoter handed him a document, showing that he was entitled to a certain number of shares of stock in a gold mine bearing the name Dolphin.

"Well, Dick," remarked his father, when Mr. Vanderhoof had left, "you are certainly getting right into business. How do you like it?"

"Very much. I only hope some of my investments pan out."

"Well, you haven't made very many, but what you have gone into you have loaded up pretty well with. However, that may be a good way. Of course, if they fail, the money loss will not make much difference to you, but I don't want to see you lose. It would show a poor head for business if you did, and I hope you haven't got that."

"So do I," remarked his son. "Oh, I'm going to make a success some way or other," and once more the vision of his uncle's home, the gloomy house set in the midst of the dark fir trees, like some residence in a cemetery, came to him as the memory of a bad dream.

"Where are you going now?" asked his father, as Dick started to leave the private office.

"I thought I'd take a ride with some of the boys in my motor boat. I haven't been out for some time."

"All right, only be careful."

"I will, dad. Good-bye."

Dick stopped, on his way home, and called for Bricktop, Frank Bender and Walter Mead, inviting them to go for a ride in his trim little craft, which was in the boat house on Lake Dunkirk.

"Let's take our lunch and stay the rest of the day," suggested Bricktop. "It's too fine out doors to be around the house."

"Good idea," assented Dick. "I'll have our cook put us up a basket of stuff."

The eyes of the other boys glistened, for they knew from experience the good things that came from the Hamilton kitchen, and they had visions of cold chicken and turkey, fine cakes and big, thick, juicy pies.

As Dick and his friends entered the side yard, they saw, standing on the driveway, a rather dilapidated wagon, drawn by a very bony horse. In the wagon was something covered with a sheet, while on the seat sat a grizzled, dried-up sort of a man, with a little bunch of whiskers on his chin. Beside him was a woman in a calico dress, and she looked worried.

"Are you Mr. Richard Hamilton?" asked the man, looking at Bricktop.

"No; he is," was the answer, and Bricktop pointed at Dick.

"Hum! Well, I'm glad to meet you. I've been waitin' some time, an' the hired man, the one with his shirt front all showin', where his vest is wore out (for thus he described the butler's dress suit), said he didn't know when you'd come home. But I brought it along with me, jest as I said I would, an' I'll show ye how it works. Mandy, jest hold th' hoss until I git th' machine out," and though the animal did not seem in need of any restraint the woman grasped the reins her husband gave her.

Then, before Dick could remonstrate, the man got down from the wagon, and began tugging at the object covered with a sheet. It seemed quite heavy.

"Would one of you young gentlemen mind givin' me a hand?" he asked, and Walter and Frank assisted him in lifting the object down to the ground.

"There ye be!" exclaimed the man, in an excited manner, while his eyes glittered in a strange way. "There she is. Now watch, everybody, when she gits goin'. Mandy, drive th' hoss up towards th' stable; it might git frightened.

"Now," he went on, "ye're about t' witness one of th' wonders of th' age. Look out, everybody!" and, with a flourish, he pulled the sheet away.

CHAPTER XIII

DICK'S BRAVE ACT

"Hold on!" cried Dick, as he saw revealed a maze of wheels, levers, belts and cranks. "What is this? Who are you?"

For an instant he thought the thing might be an infernal machine.

"Who am I?" asked the man. "Why, I'm Silas Kendall, of Manlius Centre, an' this is my perpetual motion machine. Wait until I take th' chain off so's it can git inter motion an' ye'll open yer eyes, I reckon."

"Is it dangerous?" asked Bricktop, preparing to run.

"Not a bit, if ye don't put yer fingers in th' wheels. It wouldn't harm a baby."

He drew from his pocket a key, which he proceeded to insert into a big lock that held together the ends of a chain which was twisted about the biggest wheel on the machine.

"Have t' keep it chained up," he said, with a queer sort of smile, "or it would keep on workin' all th' while. I'll show ye—Silas Kendall—he'll astonish th' world. Ye got my letter, I reckon," turning to Dick.

"Letter? No. What letter?"

"Th' one I writ ye about this machine."

"I don't remember—oh, yes," added Dick, quickly. He did recall among the many letters he had received recently (begging epistles most of them), one in which the writer said he would soon call to exhibit a new machine he had invented, and one which was destined to make all interested in it rich for life. But Dick thought it was just like lots of other missives he had been receiving from cranks since the advent of his wealth, and he threw it away. Now, it seemed, the letter was from Mr. Kendall.

"Is that really a perpetual motion machine?" asked Frank, who, with the other boys, was much interested in such things.

"Of course it is," replied the man. "I invented it all by myself. I'll tell ye a little about it before I unchain th' critter an' let it git t' work. Did ye fasten th' hoss, Mandy?" he asked, as his wife approached.

"Yep, Silas. Now, do be careful of that contraption. I ain't got no faith in it," she said, turning to the boys.

"No, that's jest th' way with wimmin," remarked Silas. "Yet I really invented it for her."

"How?" asked Dick.

"Wa'al, I was watchin' her churn one day, an' I thought how awful it was that wimmin had t' work so hard. So I decided, if I could invent a machine that would do th' work it would be a great labor-savin' device. Wa'al, I went t' work on it——"

"An' he never give up fer a year," interrupted his wife. "He neglected th' farm until it ain't worth shucks. He spent all he had saved up t' buy machinery, an' he ain't hardly slept nights with worryin' over perpetual motion. I wish he'd throw it away an' go back t' farmin'. He made money that way."

"Farmin's too hard work, Mandy," joined in Mr. Kendall. "We'll be rich now, fer this machine is destined t' revolutionize th' world. I come, jest as I writ ye," he went on, turning to Dick, "t' give ye th' fust chance t' git stock in th' new company I'm goin' t' form t' make th' machines. They don't cost much, and we'll be millionaires in a year. If you've got a leetle t' invest you'll git big dividends out of this."

"Let's see how it works," suggested Walter.

"All right," assented Silas. "I'm goin' t' unchain th' perpetual motion machine. She'll begin t' whizz as soon as I take th' shackles off, an' then—wa'al, watch out, that's all."

He sprung open the padlock with a click and the chain rattled to the ground. As it did so Mr. Kendall sprang back, as though the machine might bite him. He stooped down and peered toward it as if it might spring at him. But nothing happened. The machine was as motionless as a hitching post.

"Hum! Suthin's wrong," murmured the inventor. "Guess it got a leetle stiff comin' over in th' wagon. I'll jest give it a start. Where's a pole? Mandy, git me a clothes pole."

His wife went to the back yard, where she had noticed some, and while she was gone the boys looked at the apparatus.

It consisted of a big wheel, with spokes made in zig-zag fashion. The spokes were shaped like a trough and contained a number of metal balls, which were prevented from falling out, as the wheel turned, by some strips of wood.

There were other smaller wheels connected with the big one, and a tall chute, with a sort of endless chain, to which were attached hooks and buckets. There were also several heavy springs.

"Ye see th' way it works," explained Mr. Kendall, "is by them balls. They roll down the spokes of th' wheel, toward the tire, so t' speak, an', of course, their weight makes th' wheel go 'round. Then, when they git t' th' end of th' spokes they drop out an' roll toward th' high chute. Soon as th' balls git thar th' endless chain an' th' hooks an' buckets on it catches hold of th' balls an' lifts 'em t' th' top. Then they drop inter th' hollow spokes agin an' th' same process goes on over agin. It goes on forever, like th' brook that poetry feller writ about—I forgit his name. It's perpetual motion as sure as ye're a foot high. Ah, here comes Mandy with th' clothes pole. Now I'll jest give th' big wheel a start, 'count of it gittin' stuck, an' you'll see suthin' worth watchin'."

With the long clothes pole Silas gave the big wheel a cautious poke. It began to move slowly, and he released a big spring.

"Stand back, everybody!" he called. "She vibrates suthin' terrible when she gits goin', an' I don't want nobody t' git hurt!"

At first the wheel barely turned. Silas gave it another prod with the clothes pole and it moved more quickly. Then it released another spring and began to gather speed. Faster and faster it went, the iron balls rolling along the hollow spokes and dropping out with a noise like distant thunder.

"There she goes!" cried the old man, his chin whiskers vibrating in the intensity of his excitement. "There she goes!"

Faster and faster the wheel whizzed around. The balls began dropping with such a continuous noise that one had to shout to be heard.

"How do you stop it?" called Dick.

"No, it won't stop," replied Mr. Kendall, misunderstanding the question.

"Well, how you going to get it home?" shouted Bricktop.

"Oh, when I want to stop it I jest throw th' chain at it, an' it tangles up in th' wheel, an' slows up enough so I can fasten it. If I didn't it would go on—forever—jest like that there brook."

The machine did seem to be working well, although only on account of the strong springs. The balls, as they rolled down the inclined spokes, imparted a swift motion to the wheel. The released balls ran down an incline to the foot of the chute, and the lifting belt began to slowly turn over on the wheels on which it worked. Then something happened.

Whether Silas had not built his machine strong enough to stand the strain, or whether the perpetual motion was too much for it, was never disclosed. At any rate, when the big wheel was revolving at a rapid rate, and the balls were dropping out like immense hail stones, there was a sudden rending, splitting, breaking and cracking of wood. Then the machine seemed to creak and groan in agony. Next there was a snapping sound and the air was filled with a shower of black iron balls, as though a bombshell had burst.

"Duck, everybody!" yelled Dick. "The thing's exploded!"

The machine fairly flew apart, splinters of wood, bits of iron, belts, spokes, chute, inclines and everything was scattered to the thirty-two points of the compass.

"Oh, Silas!" exclaimed Mrs. Kendall. "There it goes!"

"Yep," answered Silas, as he ran to get under a tree. "Thar she goes, sure enough, Mandy!"

There sounded dull thuds as the balls struck the earth. Fortunately no one was hit. Then it began to rain bits of wood.

"I guess it's all over," said Dick, as he and his chums looked down from the porch where they had taken refuge. "What happened, Mr. Kendall?"

"Everything," replied the inventor, in gloomy tones. "I see what th' matter was. Th' big wheel was too strong for th' rest of th' machine. Them balls give it too much power an' it jest naturally went to flinders. I see my mistake now. I'll build it all of iron next time. Wa'al, they say experience teaches us, an' this sure has been a great experience!"

"It sure has, Silas," remarked his wife. "You'd better give it up now, an' go back t' farmin'. That'll pay."

"No, sir," replied Silas, firmly. "I'm goin' t' make a perpetual motion machine before I die, an' don't ye forgit it. I see where I made a mistake an' I'll profit by it. I don't s'pose ye'll want t' invest any thin' in it until I make my new model?" he asked Dick.

"No, I think not," answered the millionaire's son.

"Wa'al, I'll call on ye agin when I git it rebuilt," promised Silas, as he piled the bits of his broken machine into the wagon and drove off.

"Say, Dick, what'll it be next?" asked Walter, as they watched the disappointed farmer driving away. "I never knew it was so exciting to be rich."

"Oh, it's exciting, all right," answered Dick, and he added: "I don't think that was a real perpetual motion machine. The springs made it work. But, come on, or it will be too late for our motor boat ride."

With a big basket, filled with good things to eat, which the cook obligingly put up for them, the four boys were soon at the dock where Dick's craft was moored.

"Let's go to Handell's Island," proposed Bricktop. "I heard there was a cave there that no one ever got to the end of."

"That'll be fun. We'll explore it," said Dick, always ready for any sort of an adventure.

Heading the boat toward the island, which was about ten miles away, the boys stretched out on the cushions to enjoy the trip. It was a beautiful July day, hot enough to make a ride on the lake the height of enjoyment.

They reached the island in quick time, for the boat was a fast one, but, to their disappointment, the cave did not prove so mysterious as they had hoped. They managed to get to the end of it, though the way was choked with dirt and rocks, and found nothing of interest.

"This cave is a regular lemon," announced Bricktop.

"What did you hope for? To find some of Captain Kidd's treasure?" asked Walter.

"Well, it might have been used by the Indians once," was the red-haired youth's answer. "Some day I'm going to bring a lantern and see if I can't find a few arrow heads or the graves of some dead Indians."

In spite of their disappointment, the boys managed to have a good time, to which the fine lunch added not a little. It was getting dusk when they started for home, with Dick at the steering wheel.

As they approached the dock at Hamilton Corners they saw, when a mile away, that the lake in the vicinity of the boat-house was lighted up.

"What's going on?" asked Walter.

"Oh, it's carnival night," replied Dick. "I forgot all about it. They're going to have a procession of boats on the lake. We'll hurry up and join in. I wish I'd thought to decorate my boat."

He speeded up the craft, anxious, as were the other boys, to take part in the water pageant. They bore down on a little fleet of boats, gaily decorated, and filled with merry, laughing, young persons. The procession was just forming.

Suddenly there sounded a sharp report aboard Dick's boat.

"The motor back-fired," he said. "Take the wheel, Walter, while I look after it."

But, a moment later, it was seen that it was no mere back-fire in a cylinder. A sheet of flame arose from the bottom of the craft.

"The gasolene tank has exploded!" yelled Dick. "Jump for your lives, boys! The boat's afire!"

Above the hissing, crackling flames the motor still puffed away, sending the boat straight toward a confused flotilla of other craft, the occupants of which set up screams of terror as they saw what had happened.

"Jump!" cried Dick again, as he crawled aft and tried to shut off the engine.

Three splashes in the water told that his companions had leaped overboard and were comparatively out of danger.

"Come on, Dick!" cried Bricktop, rising to the surface. "Jump, or you'll be burned to death."

"I can't!" yelled back Dick, shielding his face from the awful flames with his arm. "I've got to shut off the engine, or the boat'll run into some other one and set it afire!"

Once more he bravely tried to work his way to the engine. He could not reach the gasolene cock from where he was. He cast a look ahead, and saw that his boat was approaching, at swift speed, a knot of other boats, the steersmen of which were too confused to know what to do. Some were getting out of the way, but others were in the direct course of the burning craft.

"What can I do?" Dick asked himself in a hoarse whisper. "I must stop the boat, or steer it out of the way—but how?"

He could neither reach the engine nor the wheel, for the fire was now raging in bow and stern. He stood in a little cockpit amidships, where, for the moment, there were no flames.

Dick looked desperately about him. Nearer and nearer his craft shot to the boats containing girls in their light summer dresses. Once the burning motor boat touched the craft in which the young women were their clothes would envelop them in flames.

"I must stop my boat!" thought Dick, desperately.

Then a brilliant idea came to him. He gave one look at the whirring fly-wheel of the motor. Then, seizing a heavy monkey wrench he opened the jaws and fastened it on a boat hook, so that it stood at right angles to it. Then he thrust the wrench right into the fly-wheel.

There was a grinding, crashing sound, and, a moment later, the whizzing wheel spokes had caught the wrench, and, with resistless force, had driven it through the bottom of the craft.

Dick had scuttled his own boat!

CHAPTER XIV

DICK GIVES A PARTY.

Lurching to one side, as the water rushed in through the ragged hole in the bottom, the boat, with Dick in it, began to lose headway. The water acted as a brake, and, so large was the opening the wrench had torn, that, in a few seconds, all danger was past of the burning boat colliding with other craft, the steersmen of which were too bewildered to get out of the course.

Foot by foot the scuttled boat sank. The water covered the engine now, but the motor still kept going, for enough gasolene remained in the pipe running from the exploded tank to keep it in motion. But the boat was merely floating along, all speed gone.

"Jump, Dick!" cried Bricktop, who, with the other boys, was swimming toward shore. "Jump!"

Dick stood up in the boat he had sacrificed to save the lives of others. The water was up to his knees, and, casting a look about him, he prepared to leap overboard. There was no furtherneed of his remaining, as his brave deed had accomplished what he intended it should.

But now a new danger was presented. The blazing gasolene, forced from the bottom of the boat by the rising water that came through the jagged hole, was floating on the surface of the lake. All about the sinking craft was a pool of flame, ten feet in diameter.

A cry of horror arose from those in the surrounding boats that had quickly congregated near the scene. The gathering dusk was lighted up by the licking tongues of flame, which hissed hungrily, as though angry at being cheated of their prey.

"Wait!" called a man in a large motor boat. "I'll see if I can't get near enough to save you."

He started to steer his craft toward Dick, but the latter cried out:

"No! Keep away. The gasolene is spreading! I'll jump!"

He was standing on the gunwale of the boat now, that part alone being above water. The motor had stopped, and the boat was floating amid a small sea of flame. In just the little patch where Dick stood there was, for the present, at least, no fire.

Dick crouched for a spring. He saw a place where the surrounding ring of flame was the thinnest, and he aimed for that. He was going to try to jump across the belt of fire.

Suddenly he straightened up. Then, with a spring, which lost much of its power because of the uncertain footing the tilting gunwale gave him, he launched himself upward and outward.

Arching his hands over his head to cleave the water, and hoping in his heart that he would clear the ring of flames, Dick felt himself moving through the air. Then, with a sudden change in the little breeze that was blowing, the flames shifted so that they were wider in extent at the place for which he aimed. Those in the outer fringe of motor boats caught their breaths as they saw what had happened. Dick was headed for the center of a leaping mass of fire.

An instant later he had struck the water, covered with the blazing gasolene, and had disappeared beneath the surface.

"Now to save him, if we can!" cried Captain Bailey, of the large motor boat *Cypress*, as he urged his craft forward. Those in it, as they approached the outer ring of fire, looked at the luridly illuminated waters, anxious to catch the first glimpse of Dick. A dark body came to the surface. Two hands shot out, and Dick made an attempt to swim. But he ceased almost as soon as he made the first strokes, and sank back, his head going beneath the waves.

Then sounded a splash from the stern of the boat.

"What was that?" cried Captain Bailey.

"Chandler Norton leaped after him!" was the answer.

And it was Bricktop who, in swimming to shore, had been picked up by the *Cypress*, and who had leaped after Dick when he saw him sink back. Bricktop had removed most of his heavy clothing and shoes, and was more prepared than any of the others to attempt a rescue.

It seemed a very long time that both he and Dick were lost to view, but it was only a few seconds ere Bricktop arose to the surface, one arm about the unconscious form of the millionaire's son.

"Help me get him aboard!" Bricktop gasped. "I'm afraid something has happened to him!"

Willing hands were extended to raise the silent form. Then, when the brave rescuer had been pulled over the stern, all speed was made to shore, which the other two boys had reached some time since in boats that picked them up.

Fortunately there was, in the gathering of merrymakers, a physician, who at once hurried to Dick's side. He carefully examined the youth.

"I'm afraid he inhaled some of the flames," he said, "or he may have struck his head on something when he went overboard. We must get him home, and into bed, as soon as possible."

There were several automobiles at the lake front, and in one of these Dick was taken to the Hamilton mansion at a speed which broke the law—but no one minded that.

Mr. Hamilton was much startled, but he calmly gave orders to have his son cared for. Another physician was summoned, and the two worked over the unconscious form together, while Mr. Hamilton, his face drawn and white, paced anxiously up and down in the hall outside the room.

Suddenly there sounded the patter of feet on the stairs, and, a moment later, something was muzzling Mr. Hamilton's legs, while a gentle whine begged his attention.

"What is it, Grit, old boy?" he asked, huskily, as he reached over and patted the big bulldog's head. "You know something's wrong, don't you? Well—maybe it—maybe it will be all right."

The dog whined and sniffed at the door of the room where the unconscious form of his master lay.

"No—no—not now, Grit, old boy," said Mr. Hamilton, softly, and Grit with a look as much as to say that he knew what was going on, stretched out—a grim guardian at the portal of the silent chamber.

Then, from the room, came a voice, at the sound of which the dog gave a joyous bark, and then, as though conscious that he had done wrong, he changed it to a whine. Mr. Hamilton, with wildly beating heart, heard his son murmur:

"Oh, it's cold, so cold! Where am I? Is the fire out? Did I run down any boats?"

Then came the calm voices of the doctors, urging their patient to be quiet.

But this was more than Grit could do. His whining was like the cry of a child, and he scratched frantically at the door.

"That's Grit. Let him in," Dick said, in stronger tones, and Mr. Hamilton uttered a silent prayer of thanksgiving. The portal was swung and Grit bounded into the room, followed by the millionaire. One of Dick's hands hung over the side of the bed, and Grit began licking it frantically.

"Good—old Grit," murmured Dick, and Grit was content.

"How is he?" asked Mr. Hamilton, in a whisper.

"I'm all right, dad," answered Dick, unexpectedly.

"Not as bad as we feared," answered one of the physicians. "He has inhaled no flames, but he struck his head on something as he jumped. Probably on a bit of floating wreckage. He will be all right after a few days' rest. But he must be kept quiet. No excitement. I congratulate you on your brave son, Mr. Hamilton."

The millionaire silently wrung the hand the physician held out to him.

"It wasn't anything," murmured Dick, in sleepy tones. "I had to stop the boat, and the only way I saw was to put a hole in the bottom. Too bad; it was a fine boat."

"You can have another, if we can't raise her," interrupted Mr. Hamilton.

"Then I knew I'd have to swim under water to avoid the flames," went on Dick. "I held my breath as long as I could, and then I hit something. I can't remember any more."

He sank into a doze, with Grit still licking the drooping hand.

"I think he will sleep now," said the physician who had examined Dick at the lake. "We will go out, and the dog had better come, too."

"Come, Grit," called Mr. Hamilton, but Grit paid no attention.

"I'll bring him," said the physician, as he reached for the bulldog's collar. Grit growled menacingly.

"Better not," advised the millionaire. "No one but Dick can do anything with him."

So they had to leave Grit there, but he was not in the least in the way, being content to rest beneath the bed, though whenever anyone—nurse or doctor—approached, the dog was ever on the watch.

Dick had to stay in bed three days, and for three days more was a sort of semi-invalid in an easy-chair. Then, the physicians having pronounced all danger past, he was allowed to go out. In the meantime the motor boat was raised and taken away to be repaired.

"Say, I never knew what nice sunshine and fine air we had in this town," said the youth to his father, as he walked down the street with him. "It's worth while being under the weather a bit just to appreciate it when you get out."

"I never knew you had so many friends, Dick," answered his father.

"Friends? How?"

"Why, we had to keep one of the maids busy answering the bell while you were in bed. I guess every boy, and lots of the girls, in Hamilton Corners called to see how you were getting on."

"I'm glad they thought of me," replied the millionaire's son. "I wish I could show I appreciate it."

"Well, I think you can, Dick."

"How?"

"I was going to suggest that you hold a little reception—give a sort of party. That's what we called 'em when I was a boy."

"The very thing!" exclaimed Dick. "That will be sport. But—where could I have it?"

"In the house, of course. Isn't it large enough?"

"That's just it. It's too big and fine. I'm afraid some of the boys wouldn't have a good time, for fear of dropping some cake or ice-cream on the carpets."

"Well, what would you suggest? You might give it in the barn."

"I was thinking of hiring a big tent and having a party out doors on the lawn. That would be unconventional and rather jolly, I think."

"Good idea," answered the millionaire. "I'll order a tent at once and see to the refreshments."

"Let me do that," begged Dick. "I know what boys and girls like to eat."

"Very well," assented his father, with a laugh. "You can do just as you please, and—er—send the bills to me."

"Not much!" exclaimed Dick, proudly. "I'm paying my own way now."

A week later a big white tent was erected on the spacious lawn at the Hamilton mansion. Dick had spent a busy seven days in making the arrangements, and every boy and girl in Hamilton Corners, whom Dick had the least acquaintance with, was invited.

Seldom had there been so much excitement in the town, not even when the circus came, for on this occasion the girls, at least, could "dress up," and we all know what that means to a girl. Nor were the boys behindhand in looking over their best suits and putting an extra shine on their shoes.

The big tent was gay with Chinese lanterns, and a corps of white-suited waiters were in attendance to dispense the good things when, as darkness began to gather, the young people of the town began to assemble at the party. They came from all directions, some of them awkward and shy, for it was their first big affair, while others were more self-possessed.

"Well, are you ready?" asked Simon Scardale, as he called at Guy Fletcher's house, for both had been invited to the gathering.

"Yes, but I don't care much about going. We'll have a slow time."

"Maybe we will, but I've got a little thing I want to plan out, and I can do it there, I think. The fact is, I need money badly, and I've got to get some."

"I hope you're not going to rob the house," remarked Guy, with a nervous laugh.

"Of course not, but I've got a scheme that may work. Come along."

CHAPTER XV

THE CONSPIRACY

Dick stood at the entrance to the tent receiving his guests. He was a little pale from his recent experience, but otherwise did not seem to have suffered any ill effects.

"Well, Bricktop," he called heartily, as the sandy-haired youth approached, his face almost the color of his locks, "I was afraid you wouldn't come. If it hadn't been for Bricktop there wouldn't have been any party here to-night," he went on, turning to a group of young people. "No, nor any Dick Hamilton, either. He pulled me out in the nick of time."

"Oh, pshaw! I didn't do anything," protested Bricktop, who hated praise.

"I think he was perfectly splendid!" exclaimed Mabel Ford, looking at Bricktop with her big blue eyes in a way that made that modest hero blush more fiercely than before.

"It was perfectly grand!" declared Bertha Lee, known as "Birdy" among her friends. "How I wish I was a big, strong young man," and she gazed admiringly at Bricktop.

"Why not a strong lady," suggested Simon Scardale, with a grin, as he joined the group.

At his approach several girls moved away, as they did not like him. Guy was close in Simon's wake, and both boys nodded to Dick.

"Feeling pretty fit now, old chap?" asked Simon.

"Oh, I'm all right," answered Dick.

"Feel like having a game of billiards?" went on Simon. "I'll bet you ten dollars I can beat you on your own table."

"No, thank you," replied Dick, with a laugh. "I'm too busy looking after my guests to-night. Besides, I don't play for money. Come over some other time and I'll play you all you like, for fun."

"Stingy beast," muttered Simon, as Dick moved away to greet some newcomers, "and I need the money, too."

"Maybe you'd lose," suggested Guy.

"I don't play to lose," replied Simon, with an ugly leer.

The little feeling of strangeness which many of the boys and girls at first experienced gradually wore off, and soon the party was in full swing. All sorts of games were played, and Dick and his closest chums saw to it that there was no lack of liveliness. A number of the fathers and mothers of the younger children had accompanied them, and to these older folks Dick was attentive, seeing that they had seats, and sending the waiters to them to ask if they wouldn't have a cup of coffee or some ices before supper was served.

"Say," observed one man to his wife, after Dick had found them chairs, "you'd never know he was a millionaire, would you?"

"Why not?"

"Why, because he's just like other boys—he's like one of our own folks."

"Of course he is," answered his wife. "It's only the wrong kind of people that money makes any difference to. Dick Hamilton can't help being nice. His money hasn't spoiled him," which view was shared by more than one that night.

And such a supper as there was! Long years afterward some of the boys and girls, who were quite small when they attended Dick's party, used to tell of it as though it was a visit to fairyland. Dick fairly outdone himself in seeing that everyone had a good time, and from the faces around the long tables, set within the tent, it was evident that the way to young people's hearts, or, at least, to their good spirits, is through their stomachs.

Dick walked about, like a perfect host, seeing that everyone was served, before sitting down himself. At his heels followed Grit, who was unhappy when away from his master.

"Oh, what a perfect darling of a dog!" exclaimed Birdy Lee, as she stopped over to pat Grit, which indignity he suffered in disdainful silence.

"Isn't he sweet!" chorused several other girls.

"Well, he's no beauty, judged by young ladies' standards," said Dick, with a gallant look at his girl friends. "But beauty in a bulldog is more than skin deep," he added. "Grit is pure gold when it comes to being a friend."

"What makes his two teeth stick up that way? Don't they hurt his lip?" asked Alice.

"I never heard him complain," replied Dick. "But I'd better move along, I guess. Grit is getting hungry, and I don't want him to begin on any of the waiters. He doesn't take to colored men very well. One of them started to run when Grit growled at him a while ago as the man was bringing in a roast chicken."

After supper there were more games, and the fun increased as the hours passed. Dick was congratulated on every side, not only for the success of his party, but on his speedy recovery from the boat accident.

As the millionaire's son was crossing the tent, with Grit following at his heels, he met Guy and Simon, who had been together all the evening, and who had not mingled much with the other guests.

"Hello, Grit, old boy!" exclaimed Simon, but the dog must have detected the insincerity in the youth's tones, for he uttered a low growl and showed his strong teeth.

"Oh, I'm not going to hurt you," sneered Simon.

"No, I don't think it would be exactly healthy," remarked Dick.

"Is he a very valuable dog?" Simon went on, paying no further attention to Grit.

"Well, he's rated at a thousand dollars in the records of the Kennel Club," answered Dick. "I don't know that any dog is worth so much from a financial standpoint, but I know I wouldn't sell him for that; would I, Grit?" and the bulldog almost wagged his stump of a tail off in delight at Dick's caressing words.

"Humph! I'd look at a thousand dollars a good while before I'd give it for a dog," cried Simon.

"You don't know Grit," was Dick's quiet answer, as he turned away.

"Come on, Guy," said Simon, a little later. "I'm going to clear out of here."

"What for? Let's have some more ice-cream. It's bully."

"No," replied Simon, shortly. "I've got a scheme on for making some money out of Dick, and taking him down a peg. I owe him something for spoiling that bond sale."

"But he didn't spoil it," replied Guy, who, in spite of certain mean traits of character, was inclined to be fair. "Besides, you wouldn't have sold Dick worthless bonds, would you?"

"How was I to know they were worthless?" asked Simon, with a short laugh. "He has to take chances in this world. But this time there'll be no slip-up. Come on, I've got to see a man to-night."

As the two walked from the tent, where the merry-making was still going on, Guy saw something dangling from Simon's pocket. It looked like a small black snake.

"What's that?" he asked, in some alarm.

"Hush!" whispered Simon. "That's the leash thong of Dick Hamilton's bulldog. Come along!"

CHAPTER XVI

DICK TURNS DETECTIVE

"Well, Dick," remarked Mr. Hamilton at breakfast the next morning, "your party was a great success."

"I hope they all had a good time. They seemed to. I know I did."

"Yes, they were a fine lot of young people," went on the millionaire. "Oh, by the way, I had a letter from the man in Yazoo City I wrote to about your gold mine stock. Nick Smith, his name is. He's an old forty-niner, I understand."

"What does he say?"

"The mine is all right. He sent me a report from the government assay office, and I guess the Dolphin is as good as the Hop Toad."

"Then I'd better finish paying for the stock when Mr. Vanderhoof comes to town again," said Dick. "It will be mine then, and all I'll have to do is to wait for it to increase and pay me big dividends."

"I hope it does," answered Mr. Hamilton. "I also had a letter from Vanderhoof yesterday. He also had heard from Smith, it appears, and as he learned the mine was favorably reported on, he sent word that he'd call to-day for the fifteen hundred dollars."

"He can have it, dad," said Dick. "I guess I'll go down to the bank with you. What time will Mr. Vanderhoof be there?"

"At eleven, his letter said. Well, if you have finished breakfast, come along. You're getting to be quite a financier."

"I'm going to make that a paying investment if it's a possible thing," answered Dick, as he walked through the well-kept grounds toward the street and thought of Uncle Ezra's place.

Mr. Vanderhoof was promptly on time, and had the bonds ready for Dick, who paid for them with a check. The youth, who had about given up trying to recall where he had seen Vanderhoof before, thought the mining promoter smiled more than ever like a cat as he handed over the securities and took the money.

"I'm sure I hope you double your capital," he remarked, with a smirk that showed nearly all his teeth.

"Oh, if I make twenty-five per cent. I'll be satisfied," answered Dick.

"Well, I'll be in town for a few days," Mr. Vanderhoof went on, "and if either of you would like to take some more mining stock I'll be glad to accommodate you."

"I have enough," replied the millionaire, and Dick answered that he wanted to see how this investment turned out before venturing another.

"Well, I'll be in town, at any rate," was the promoter's parting remark.

Dick felt quite like a man of business as he looked over his check book a little later and noted what he had paid out. True, he had taken in nothing since he had come into his fortune, but he knew the wealth his mother had left him was accumulating interest all the while—faster, in fact, than he had spent it so far. Still he wished that he was receiving an income from some efforts of his own.

"Never mind, wait until my stock in the gold mine and the milk company begins to boom," he told himself. "That is, if that milk concern doesn't demand another assessment," he added, dubiously.

Dick walked slowly home, and, passing around the side of the house, approached the stable. He intended taking a gallop on Rex that afternoon and wanted the groom to have the horse in readiness. As he neared Grit's kennel he noticed that the chain was thrown over the top of the house, as it usually was when the dog was loose.

"Where's Grit?" he asked of Peters, the groom.

"Grit, Master Dick?" inquired the man, in great surprise. "Sure an' didn't you send for him about an hour ago?"

"Me send for him?" repeated Dick in some alarm, for Grit, even if he was unchained, would not stray away from the stable. He was nowhere in sight, and Dick at once became worried.

"Sure, Master Dick," went on the groom. "About an hour ago a youngish chap came here and said you'd sent him for Grit."

"And you let him take him?"

"Why, sure, I thought you'd sent for him, as you did once."

"Yes, but then I sent a note, Peters."

"That's so, but the young man had Grit's leash, sir; and, though the dog was inclined to be a bit ugly, he seemed to know the leash and went along after a bit."

"What sort of a man got him?" asked Dick, quietly, though he was much excited over what seemed to be the theft of his pet.

"A young man, not very nice-looking, Master Dick, and smelling very strong of the stables. In fact, that's what made Grit finally take to him. Grit's very fond of horses and stables, sir. He'll let almost anyone come near him as long as they've been around a barn."

"That's so. Did the man say anything, or give any name?"

"No. He just said you were going for a walk and wanted Grit to go 'long. Said you was too busy to come and had sent the leash so's he'd have no trouble. He didn't have—that is, not very much—barring that Grit wanted to get hold of his leg first. But when the dog had sniffed at the leash, probably knowin' it came from you, he was quiet enough. But I could see the man was askeered of him, Master Dick. He walked to one side like. Why, Master Dick, is anything wrong?"

"Wrong? I should say so! Grit's been stolen, Peters."

"You don't say so, Master Dick!" exclaimed the man, much alarmed at his part in the matter.

"Yes, he's been stolen, and by a clever trick," went on Dick. "But I don't blame you, Peters. I remember now, I lost the leash thong last night. I had it on Grit and I took it off and put it in my pocket. Then I missed it after the party, and I was too tired to look for it. Someone must have found it, and, knowing it belonged to Grit, made up his mind to steal him. The fellow must have known he'd come more willingly after smelling his own leash."

"But you must have lost it somewhere around here," went on Peters. "Someone at the party may have found it."

"If they had they would have known it was mine," answered Dick. "No, I think someone outside found it and he stole Grit. Well, I've got to find him, that's all. Saddle Rex, and I'll make some inquiries about town."

"But it's near dinner-time, Master Dick."

"I don't care. I can't eat if Grit is gone," and with a heavy heart Dick waited for the horse to be saddled. He whistled shrilly his favorite call to Grit, hoping the dog might have broken awaynot far from the stable, and be in hiding somewhere, but no Grit appeared.

On the back of Rex, Dick made a hasty tour of the immediate neighborhood, inquiring of various persons he met if they had seen the bulldog. Grit was well known about Hamilton Corners, for he was often seen in his master's company. But this time no one had noticed him being led off in leash by a young man who seemed quite afraid of the brute that was so handsome for his very ugliness.

"He's been stolen for a reward," was Mr. Hamilton's opinion when he came home to lunch and heard Dick's woeful story. "You'll hear from him sooner or later. Better advertise in the county papers."

Dick put in several notices that afternoon, offering to pay a reward of a hundred dollars for the return of Grit.

"Now we'll have to wait," said the millionaire. "Never mind, Dick; if Grit is gone you can get another dog," for Mr. Hamilton was as fond of animals as was his son.

"There'll never be another Grit," answered Dick, sorrowfully.

Meanwhile, Grit was being led across the country fields which stretched out back of the Hamilton mansion.

"I've got to keep off the roads," muttered the youth who had hold of the leash. "There's too many people as knows a dorg like this. I wish I hadn't gone into this game. It's too risky, not only at bein' caught, but I don't like the way this dorg looks at my legs. He looks hungry."

Indeed, Grit was in no amiable frame of mind. He consented to be led along because he recognized his old leash, and the man leading him had the familiar smell of horses, which Grit loved so well. The dog was a little suspicious, but once before Dick had sent a stranger for him and the man had smelled of horses, so Grit, though he had grave doubts, was willing to go along. But he was getting anxious to see his master, as his uneasy growls from time to time indicated, to the no small alarm of the somewhat ragged youth leading him.

"Easy now, old boy," he said. "That's a good dorg. We'll soon be there," he added, as he cast an uneasy look around. "The wagon must be waiting somewheres about here."

He cut through a little clump of trees and emerged upon an unfrequented road that led to Leonardville, a distant settlement.

"There's the rig!" he exclaimed, as he caught sight of a wagon and a horse hitched to the fence. "The worst of it's over."

"Did you get 'im?" asked a man in the wagon.

"Yep, an' I'll be glad to git rid of 'im. He's a little too anxious to see what my legs is made of."

Grit was led toward the wagon. He seemed to think something was not just right, for he growled menacingly and hung back.

"Hold 'im a minute now, until I git the bag," ordered the man in the wagon, and, as the ragged youth did so, the man suddenly threw a big sack over Grit's head. Then, hastily wrapping him up in it and tying several turns of rope about it, the sack and dog were tossed into the wagon.

"Quick's the word!" exclaimed the man, as he and the youth got up on the seat and drove off. "Now to get our share of the reward. I hope that young feller what put up this job knows what he's about."

Poor Grit, whining and growling alternately in the bottom of the wagon, tried to work the suffocating bag off his head, but it was too tightly fastened.

The mail the next day brought Dick a badly-written and worse-spelled missive, in which it was stated that if he wanted Grit returned he could have him by paying two hundred dollars' reward. No names were signed, and the handwriting was unfamiliar.

"I told you so," said Mr. Hamilton. "But who's got him?"

"The letter doesn't say. I'm to leave two hundred dollars to-night under a flat stone, near the stump just where the county road crosses Butternut Creek. Then, the letter says, the dog will be back at the stables to-morrow morning."

"Well," remarked Mr. Hamilton, "that's a hundred more than you advertised to pay. I guess you can't help yourself. You'd better do as the letter says."

"I'll not!" exclaimed Dick.

"What are you going to do? Inform the police? They won't be able to do much. Besides, they'll never bother over a dog, no matter how valuable he is."

"No," replied Dick. "I'm not going to tell the police."

"What then?"

"I'm going to turn detective myself and find Grit! See, here is the first clue," and he held up the envelope of the letter. "This was mailed in Leonardville. I'm going there for a starter, and I'll find Grit!"

With flashing eyes Dick hurried to the stables to order Rex saddled.

CHAPTER XVII.

GRIT'S REVENGE.

Peters soon had the horse ready, and as Dick leaped into the saddle his father came hurrying out to the stables.

"Now be careful, Dick," he cautioned. "Don't do anything rash. What are your plans?"

"I'm going to ride in the direction of Leonardville. That's about ten miles by the main road. I'll inquire as I go along; but what I'll do after I get there I can't tell."

"Well, be careful, that's all," concluded Mr. Hamilton. "The fellows who stole Grit are no common thieves, I imagine, and I hope you don't get into trouble with them."

"I'm not worrying about trouble. Once I get where Grit is, he and I can take care of the thieves all right," and Dick laughed grimly.

He started off at an easy canter, though Rex was full of mettle and wanted to gallop.

"No, Rex," said Dick, for he had a habit of talking to his horse as he did to Grit. "We'll take it easy. We've got a long day ahead of us."

It was about ten o'clock, and Dick decided to ride several miles without stopping to make inquiries, as the day previous he had pretty well covered the neighborhood near his home. But in about an hour, having reached a small village, he asked several persons he met if they had seen anything of his dog. No one had, and he pushed on.

Mile after mile he rode, stopping every little while to make inquiries, but without avail. He got dinner at a wayside hotel and then resumed his trip. It was about three o'clock when, as he stopped at a watering trough under a big chestnut tree on the edge of the road, he saw a wagon coming toward him.

"I'll ask this man," thought Dick. He waited until the vehicle and the driver were in plainer view through the cloud of dust raised and then he exclaimed:

"Why, Henry! How'd you get out here?"

"Oh, I've been after some old iron," replied the secretary and general man-of-all-work of the International and Consolidated Old Metal Corporation. "I heard of a farmer who had a lot of scrap for sale and I went after it."

"Did you get it?"

"Sure. It's in the wagon," and Henry nodded toward the rear of his vehicle, which was filled with a mass of broken iron. "I started away from home yesterday afternoon expecting to get back last night, but I had a breakdown and I had to stay until morning. But what are you doing out here?"

"Looking for Grit," and then Dick told about the theft of his dog. "I don't s'pose you've seen anything of him, have you?"

"Where did you say that letter came from?" asked Henry, showing some excitement.

"Leonardville. That's where I'm headed for. Why?"

"Then I saw your dog!" exclaimed Henry.

"Where?" asked Dick, excitedly.

"I was driving along last night," went on the young representative of the old metal concern, "and, just before I had my breakdown, I saw a wagon pass me. I looked in the back and saw something covered with a blanket. It was moving, and I wondered what it could be when I heard a dog bark. I thought it was rather funny to cover a dog up that way on a hot day. One of the men leaned back, and, when it barked, he hit the dog with a whip."

"Poor Grit!" murmured Dick. "Wait till I get hold of those fellows. Where did they go, Henry?"

"I'll tell you. I was thinking that was a pretty mean way to treat a dog, but I never thought they might have stolen him, and were trying to keep him hid. I watched their wagon until it was out of sight and then——"

"Did you lose sight of them?" broke in Dick.

"I went on a little farther," continued Henry, "and one of the springs of my wagon broke. I knew I couldn't get it fixed until morning, so I unhitched the horse and drove him along until I came to a hotel. This was at Maysville, and when I got to the tavern I saw the same two fellows. They were just driving away, and I heard one say it wasn't far to the Eagle Hotel. Now there's an Eagle hotel in Leonardville, and I'll bet you'll find your men and dog there. I'd like to go back with you and help——"

"That's all right, Henry," interrupted Dick. "I guess I can manage," and, calling back his thanks to the young iron merchant, and promising to see him later, Dick urged his horse off at a gallop, disappearing in a cloud of dust.

"Now there's a good example for you to follow, old bag of bones," said Henry, addressing his own steed. "Why don't you try that for a change and you'd get home to supper quicker. Well, I s'pose you'll last longer if you don't go so fast," and, with that comforting reflection, Henry managed, after a time, to get his horse in motion, the beast having almost gone to sleep during its driver's talk with Dick.

"Now to find Grit!" exclaimed the millionaire's son, as he galloped on. "Poor dog, I hope they haven't abused you very much."

Dick did not stop along the road to make any further inquiries. He reached Leonardville in good time and soon found his way to the Eagle Hotel. He let Rex trot into the stable yard, and,dismounting, told one of the hostlers to feed and water the animal when it had cooled off.

As Dick started up the steps to the porch, intending to make some inquiries of the landlord, he suddenly started back in surprise, for, coming out of the main entrance, was Simon Scardale.

"Hello, Simon!" exclaimed Dick.

"Why-er-w-w-why, hello—Dick," stammered Simon. "Have you come to—what are you doing here?" he managed to say, with an attempt at pleasantry.

"I might ask you the same thing," responded Dick.

But Simon did not wait to hear anything further. He darted back into the hotel murmuring:

"Wait a minute—I've forgotten something—see you right away——"

"He acts as though he was afraid to meet me," thought Dick, as he walked on. "I wonder what he's doing here?"

An instant later he was surprised to see Simon come out of a side door and fairly run to the stables. At the same instant a man appeared in the door of the barn, and to him Simon made frantic gestures to remain hidden. Then, as Dick watched this by-play with a bewildered air, there came from the stable the bark of a dog.

"Grit!" exclaimed Dick. "Grit! Grit, old boy!"

The barks became a howl of rage and there sounded the rattle of a chain.

"Grit! Grit!" cried Dick, running toward the stable.

There was the noise of a chain snapping. Then came frightened shouts. An instant later Simon, followed by a ragged man and a youth, dashed from the barn with the bulldog in close pursuit. Out of the hotel yard they raced, with Grit growling and barking and making fierce leaps for them.

"Grit!" called Dick, but, for once, Grit refused to obey his master's voice. His heart was too full of revenge for the insults he had suffered.

Out into the highway ran Simon and the two others, with the dog gaining at every leap.

"Help! Save me!" cried Simon, as Dick ran out to see what the end would be. He was fearful that Grit would get one of the fleeing ones down and set his teeth into his throat.

"Grit! Grit!" he called, frantically, but the bulldog never heeded.

Simon turned, hoping to get out of the path of the maddened beast, but he did not reckon on Grit's quickness. The dog made a grab for Simon's trousers and caught them at the seat. There was a ripping sound, a frantic yell from Simon, and he fell, rolling over and over in a cloud of dust.

"Grit! Don't bite him!" shouted Dick, fearful of what might happen.

CHAPTER XVIII.

UNCLE EZRA'S VISIT.

But Grit had no intentions of wasting time on Simon when his revenge was not complete. He dropped the large piece of cloth he had torn from Simon's trousers and kept on after the two other fleeing individuals.

The ragged youth was the faster runner, and the man, lagging behind, turned as if to beat off the dog. But Grit was fearless. Right at the man he sprang, and the fellow gave a yell of agony as he saw the brute launched at his throat. But Grit was not blood-thirsty. He caught the man by the lapel of his ragged coat, and, in an instant, had pulled him to the ground. Then, having worried him until the thief must have thought he was being eaten alive, Grit left him and set off after the third of the trio.

The youth was becoming exhausted, but Grit was as fresh as ever. There was no give-up to him. He caught the ragged lad before he had gone a hundred feet farther and soon had him down. He fairly tore the coat off his back, and, after standing over him a few seconds, growling as though he was about to tear him into little pieces, Grit, with a satisfied shake of his head, started back on the run toward Dick.

"Grit! Grit, old boy! So they tried to steal you, did they?" murmured Dick, as the dog bounded up on him and frantically licked his face. "Well, I guess they wish they hadn't."

Grit nearly shook himself apart trying to wag his stump of a tail to show his delight at again being with his master. Dick fairly hugged his pet, but the tears almost came to his eyes as he saw several cruel welts on the dog's satin-like coat, where he had been beaten.

"So they struck you, eh?" asked Dick, a fierce light coming into his brown eyes. "I don't blame you for taking after them as soon as you broke loose. I guess I'll have a score to settle with Simon and his cronies."

But there was no chance to do this. Simon gave one look at Dick and Grit as they walked back to the hotel. Then, trying to pull his coat down so as to conceal the big hole in his trousers, he hurried away up the road, after the man and youth, who had continued their interrupted escape as soon as they were assured that Grit had left each two legs on which to run.

"Well, Grit, old boy," went on Dick, as he entered the hotel. "I got you back without putting any two hundred dollars under a stone at Butternut Creek, didn't I? But I guess Henry is entitled to his hundred of the reward. Now to make some inquiries."

The landlord soon told all he knew of the case. Late the previous night, he said, the ragged youth and his companion had arrived at the hotel, bringing the dog in the wagon. They said they had purchased it and were taking it to a man in the country. They paid for the keep of themselves and their horse and remained all night.

"This morning the well-dressed young fellow came along," went on the landlord.

"That was Simon," murmured Dick.

"He registered as Thomas Henderson," said the hotel keeper. "I didn't much like his looks, but I'm here to hire rooms and furnish meals to travelers, not to criticise 'em. I was a leetle s'prised that he seemed to know them other two, but I thought that was his business. He seemed to know the dog, too, but the beast didn't take much of a notion to him. They stayed here all day, and one of my hostlers says the dog tried to break loose several times. They kept him chained in the stable, and they licked him more than once, I guess. They said he was savage and had to be beat to make him mind."

"Poor Grit," murmured Dick, and the dog barked joyfully at being again with his master.

"Wa'al," resumed the hotel man, "Simon, as you call him, an' the other two, they had several talks together. I heard 'em say suthin' about expectin' someone with money."

"That was me," interposed Dick, with a smile.

"Only I determined to get my dog, if I could, without paying them anything."

"And you did it," said the landlord, with a laugh.

"I did," replied Dick. "But I never suspected Simon would try such a desperate game as this. He must have found the leash the night of the party," he went on, after telling the landlord what had happened. "Then he got in with these fellows and had them steal Grit. The letter they mailed gave me a clue, and Henry told me enough more to enable me to find Grit. Well, I guess I've seen the last of Simon Scardale."

It was not exactly the last, but Simon did not reappear in Hamilton Corners, and, though he afterward played a part in Dick's life, he had dropped out of it for the present.

The horse and wagon, which the man and youth left behind, was called for that evening by an individual of the tramp variety, but, as he brought the cash to pay the last of the hotel bill, the landlord let him take the rig. Dick decided to stay at the Eagle Hotel all night, and he sent a telegram to his father explaining his absence and telling of his success. He decided he would not follow up Simon or his cronies to prosecute them for the theft.

As the journey was a little too long for Grit to make afoot, and as Dick could not take him in the saddle with him, he sent Rex home in care of a man he hired, and engaged a carriage for himself and the dog, arriving home the next day at noon.

"Well," remarked Mr. Hamilton, as his son came in with Grit, "your detective work was all right."

"Yes, thanks to Henry Darby," answered the son. "I'm going to send him a check for a hundred dollars," which he proceeded to do.

"Here are a couple of letters for you," went on the millionaire, handing the missives to his son. One proved to be a note from Guy Fletcher. He had heard what had occurred regarding the dog, for Mr. Hamilton told several friends of his son's telegram, and Guy hastened to assure Dick that he had no idea of Simon's scheme.

"He told me he was only going to play a joke on you," wrote Guy, in the note which was delivered by a messenger. "He took the leash from your pocket the night of the party, and said he was going to hide Grit and make you believe he was stolen. I hope you don't believe I'd have anything to do with Simon if I thought he intended to really steal your dog. He has gone out West, I hear, somewhere in the gold mine region. My father has forbidden me to ever speak to Simon again."

"I guess you'll not get a chance right away," murmured Dick.

The whole thing was plain to him now. Simon wanted money, and thought he could make it by getting the man and youth to steal Grit, and then making Dick put the two hundred dollars under the stone. Everything had gone well up to a certain point. The dog had been taken away, carried in the wagon to Leonardville, and thither Simon had gone to make the final arrangements. The unexpected appearance of Dick had spoiled the scheme. Simon had hurried to the barn to warn his confederates, but at that instant Grit, excited by a beating he was getting, had broken loose.

"No," mused Dick, "I don't believe Simon will show up around here for some time."

"Who is the other letter from?" asked Mr. Hamilton.

"I don't know. I'll open it."

Dick rapidly scanned the contents.

"Uncle Ezra Larabee is coming to pay us a visit," he announced. "He'll be here tomorrow."

"Uncle Ezra, eh?" repeated Mr. Hamilton. "I suppose he wants to see how you are getting on—with your investments."

"Hum!" exclaimed Dick, with an uneasy laugh, "maybe he thinks the year is up and I'm to go back with him. But it isn't—I'm glad to say."

"Well, we must make his visit pleasant," said Mr. Hamilton. "It isn't often he comes to Hamilton Corners."

Uncle Ezra Larabee arrived the next day. Dick was in the library reading when he heard the door bell ring and the butler answered it.

"Is Mr. Hamilton in?" he heard a voice ask, and he knew it was his uncle. The boy hastened to greet his relative.

"Why didn't you let us know what train you were coming on and I would have met you with the carriage," asked Dick, politely.

"No, thank you, Nephew Richard," replied Uncle Ezra, in rasping tones. "I'm not too old to walk, and it's well to save the horse all you can."

"And you carried that heavy valise?" asked Dick.

"Of course I did, Nephew Richard. You didn't suppose I was going to pay twenty-five cents to have a boy carry it, did you? Lots of them wanted to, but twenty-five cents isn't earned every day, so I brought it myself," and with an expression of pain that he could not conceal Mr. Larabee set the heavy satchel down. His arm was stiff from carrying it, but he smiled grimly with satisfaction when he thought of the quarter of a dollar he had saved.

"Come right upstairs and I'll show you to your room," invited Dick. "Then I'll telephone father you are here."

"No, no, don't waste any money telephoning, Nephew Richard," said Uncle Ezra, hastily.

"Why it doesn't cost anything, uncle. We have to pay for the telephone by the year."

"Well, don't do it. They might charge you something this time. You never can tell. Besides, you might interrupt your father in some business deal and make him lose some money. No, I'll wait until he comes home."

"Very well," assented Dick.

"Gracious! What's that?" exclaimed Uncle Ezra, as a low growl came from a dark corner by the stairs. "Have you any wild beasts in here?"

"No, that's only my dog, Grit, uncle. He'll not hurt anyone."

"A dog? In the house?" exclaimed Mr. Larabee. "Why, he might chew a hole in the carpet. Besides, I can't bear dogs. Get out, you brute!" he exclaimed, aiming a kick at Grit, who walked toward Dick.

The bulldog, with an ugly growl, crouched for a leap at Mr. Larabee.

CHAPTER XIX.

THE FRESH-AIR YOUNGSTERS.

"Hold him back! Hold him! Let me hide! He'll bite me!" exclaimed Uncle Ezra, as he saw Grit's wicked-looking teeth.

"Grit!" spoke Dick, softly, and in a reproving voice. "This is my Uncle Ezra," he went on. "Don't you know any better than that?"

Instantly Grit's manner changed. He showed that he was sorry for the mistake he had made of growling at one of the family visitors. He even approached Uncle Ezra as if to make friends, but Mr. Larabee shrunk away.

"I can't bear dogs," he said.

Grit acted as if he understood, for he turned away. Nor did he seem to miss a caress from Mr. Larabee. Grit was a wise dog, and he well knew that the man disliked him.

"If you keep that dog in the house I'm afraid I can't stay, Nephew Richard," Dick's uncle went on. "I wouldn't sleep a wink thinking of him."

"Gibbs, take Grit to the stable," said Dick to the butler, with a little sigh, and the dog, with a somewhat reproachful look at his master, allowed himself to be led away. Nor was he permitted to come into the house during Uncle Ezra's visit, which quarantine he seemed to resent, for he always growled menacingly whenever Mr. Larabee came near him out doors. But this was not often, as Dick's uncle was very much afraid of Grit.

Mr. Hamilton soon came home, and warmly greeted his wife's brother.

"I'm glad to see you," said the millionaire. "How would you like to take a run to Hazelton this evening to the theatre? They have a good summer company playing there and we can make a quick trip in Dick's runabout."

"I never go to theatres," said Mr. Larabee, in severe tones. "It's sinful, and a wicked waste of money. If there is a good instructive lecture in the village I would much rather go to that."

"I'm afraid there isn't," replied Mr. Hamilton, trying not to smile, for he respected his brother-in-law's scruples. "But we can spend the evening pleasantly at home—talking."

"Pleasantly!" repeated Dick to himself, with a sort of groan. "Pleasantly, with Uncle Ezra? Never!"

After supper Mr. Larabee and Dick's father chatted in the library. The talk ranged from business matters to subjects in Dankville, where Mr. Hamilton knew several families.

"Perhaps you'd like to take a look about the house," suggested Mr. Hamilton, after a pause "I've been putting in some improvements lately, and enlarging the conservatory. Dick will show you around."

"What? Tramp through the house just to look at it? I don't believe in doing that," replied Uncle Ezra, firmly. "Things wear out fast enough as it is without using them when it isn't necessary. No use walking on the best carpets when there isn't a need for it. Besides, I don't believe in spending money on a house when it's good enough. Your place was very nice without adding to it. Think of the money you could have saved."

"But I didn't have to save it," responded Mr. Hamilton. "I made lots this year, and I thought it was a wise thing to put it into something permanent. I have increased the value of my house."

"Much better put it in the bank," advised Uncle Ezra, with a disapproving sniff.

Mr. Hamilton and Dick tried to entertain their visitor, but it was hard work. He cared nothing for the things they were interested in, and was somewhat inclined to dictate what Mr. Hamilton should do with his money.

"You burn too many lights," he said, noting that several incandescents were aglow in the library where they sat. "One would do as well," and he turned out all but one.

"I contract for it by the year," said Mr. Hamilton. "It doesn't cost me any more to burn five lamps than it does one."

"But the lamps wear out," was Uncle Ezra's answer. "And speaking of things wearing out reminds me. We got a letter the other day and it almost made Samanthy sick. She hasn't got over the shock of it yet."

"What was it?" asked Dick.

"Why, it was from some crazy society in New York, wanting us to take twenty-five 'fresh-air children,' the letter said, to board at our house for a few weeks. Said they heard we had a big farmhouse and could accommodate 'em."

"Are you going to take them?" inquired Mr. Hamilton. "I think your house would be just the place for them. You have lots of room, and you can't eat all that you raise on the farm. It would do the poor things good."

"Are—we—going—to—take—them?" repeated Mr. Larabee. "I'm surprised at you, Mortimer Hamilton. The idea of taking twenty-five street-arabs in our house! Why, the very idea of it made Samanthy sick a bed for a day. Those rapscallions wouldn't leave a carpet on the floor! They'd tear the house apart! I know! I've read about 'fresh-air children' before."

"You might take the carpets up," suggested Dick, with a smile.

"What?" almost shouted Uncle Ezra. "Nephew Richard, there's carpets in our house that hasn't been up for years. Why the spare room hasn't been opened since sister Jane's funeral, and that was—let me see—that was the year when Ruth Enderby got married. Take 'fresh-air children' into our house! Why, we wouldn't have any house left at the end of the week."

"Oh, I guess not as bad as that," replied Mr. Hamilton, indulgently. "But, of course, you know your own business best. I hope Mrs. Larabee soon recovers."

"She may, but it was quite a shock," replied Uncle Ezra. "Well, I think I'll go to bed. I must be up early in the morning. I came here to transact a little business, and the sooner it's over the sooner I can get back home. I'm afraid my hired man will burn too much kindling wood starting the fires. He's the most wasteful man I ever saw." And, sighing deeply at the depravity of hired men in general and his own in particular, Uncle Ezra went to bed.

Dick offered to take him for a spin in the runabout the next day, but his uncle declined, on the ground that there might be an accident.

"You might run somebody down and hurt them," he said. "Then they'd sue you for damages and I'd be liable for a share. I haven't any money to throw away on automobile accidents."

"All right," said Dick. "But I'm very careful."

"You can come walking with me instead," suggested his uncle. "You and I ought to be friends. We may have to live together some day, you know," and he tried to smile, but it was only a forced grin.

"Not much!" thought Dick, as, with rather a heavy heart, he prepared to accompany his uncle on the walk. "No, no, Grit, you can't go," he said, as the dog jumped about in delightful anticipation, for he always went with Dick. "You might bite Uncle Ezra," he added, as, much against his wish, he chained Grit in the kennel. Dick could not bear to look back at his pet, who gazed reproachfully after him.

Dick showed his uncle such sights as there were in Hamilton Corners. It was a hot day, and, as they tramped along, Dick got quite thirsty.

"Come in here, Uncle Ezra," he suggested, as they passed a drug store, "and we'll get some soda water."

"What? Pay for a drink of water?" asked Mr. Larabee, horrified.

"Well, it's got ice-cream in it," replied Dick.

"It's a sinful waste of money!" declared his uncle. "We can get all the water we want to drink at home. But, as I am a little thirsty, I'll go in and ask the man for a glass of plain water. He'll be glad to give it to us."

Dick was a little doubtful on this score, and he felt that it would be rather embarrassing to have his uncle ask for water in the drug store, where Dick was well known. But he was too polite to object to what Mr. Larabee did. The latter walked into the store, and, in his rasping voice, asked for two glasses of water.

"Do you mean soda water?" inquired the clerk.

"No, plain water. I don't drink such trash as soda water," replied Mr. Larabee.

The clerk looked at him in much astonishment, and then glanced at Dick. The latter managed to wink, and the clerk seemed to understand. He went to the back part of the store, and presently came back with two glasses of water.

"There, nephew," said Mr. Larabee, triumphantly, as he sipped the plain beverage. "You see our thirst is quenched and we have saved our money. Young men should economize, and when they are old they will not want."

"Yes, sir," replied Dick, dutifully, but when they went out he managed to lay ten cents on the counter where the clerk would see it. Dick wasn't going to be made fun of the next time he went in for a glass of soda.

"Now, I think we'll go home, Nephew Richard," suggested Mr. Larabee, when they had walked an hour longer. "There is no use wearing out our shoes any more than we can help. Besides, I have some business to transact this afternoon, and I must get the papers out of my valise."

Dick was glad enough to return, and gladder still, when, the next morning, Uncle Ezra announced that he was going back to Dankville.

"You must come and see me and your Aunt Samantha," he said to Dick, as he bade the lad good-bye, and Dick murmured something that might be taken as an expression of a fervent desire to pay another visit to The Firs, but it was not.

"Dad," said Dick that night, "do you know what I'm thinking of?"

"Not exactly, you think of so many things."

"I'm thinking of those poor little fresh-air kids, and how disappointed they must be not to get a trip to the country. I don't know as I want them to go to Uncle Ezra's, but—er—say, dad, I'd like to give a bunch of fresh-air kids some sort of an outing. Think of the poor little tots shut up in sizzling New York this kind of weather."

"Well, you can bring them here, I suppose," began Mr. Hamilton, doubtfully, with a look around his handsomely furnished house, "only this isn't exactly the country."

"Oh, I didn't mean here," said Dick, hastily. "I was thinking we could have a crowd of 'em out to Sunnyside."

This was the name of a large farm which Mr. Hamilton owned on the outskirts of the country village of Prattville.

"The very thing!" exclaimed Mr. Hamilton, with as much fervor as Dick had shown. "That's the ticket, Dick. I'll write to Foster at once and ask him if he and his wife can take a crowd of the waifs at Sunnyside for a few weeks. Then you will have to manage the other end yourself. Foster will do as I say, I guess, for he loves children and he has a heart as big as a barrel. You'll have to furnish the children."

"I'll do it!" exclaimed Dick, delightedly. "I'll write to Uncle Ezra and ask him the address of that committee in New York. Hurrah for the fresh-air kids! I hope they have a good time!"

"I guess they will if he has anything to do with it," mused Mr. Hamilton, with a fond look at his son as Dick went to get writing material to pen a letter to Uncle Ezra.

CHAPTER XX

TIM'S DISCLOSURE

Two days later Dick received a reply from Mr. Larabee. In the meanwhile Mr. Hamilton had written to Foster, the man he hired to take charge of Sunnyside farm, and had told him to have the place in readiness for twenty-five youngsters.

"Did your Uncle Ezra give you the address of the Fresh-Air Committee?" asked Dick's father.

"Yes, and he sent me a letter of advice along with it."

"What does he say?"

"I'll read it to you," and Dick turned over the pages of the missive. "This is what he says about my plan of trying to give those kids a little fun:

"'I send you the address of the committee, as you requested, but, Nephew Richard, I want to warn you against taking them. In the first place, they will be no better off than they are at home. They will not appreciate what you do for them. Then, too, they might bring some terrible epidemic to this part of the country. Sunnyside is not so far from Dankville but that a disease might carry to my place, and you know my health is not strong.

"'If I had control of you (as I may have some day), I would not let you do this. But it is not for me to say at this time what you should do. I think you are throwing the money away, and you had much better put the amount you intend spending into the church missionary box and so aid the heathens. They need it.'

"As if those poor kids in the hot tenements of New York didn't need it, too," commented Dick. "Well, Uncle Ezra is certainly a queer man. I suppose he'll keep his house filled with disinfectants while the waifs are at Sunnyside, though it's many miles away."

In about a week Dick had completed arrangements with the committee in New York, the president of which wrote to thank him for aiding in the work they were doing. Dick was told that twenty-five youngsters, ten boys and fifteen girls, none of whom had ever been to the country before, would be sent to Sunnyside in charge of a matron. Dick had forwarded money to buy the tickets, and had planned with Foster to have a big stage meet the train on which the "fresh-air kids," as he called them, would arrive at the nearest station to the country home.

"Well, dad," remarked Dick, the day before the waifs from New York were to arrive, "you've seen the last of me for a week."

"Why; where are you going?"

"To Sunnyside. I want to see that the kids are started right, and I think I'll stay about a week to see that they have a good time. I'll take my runabout, and I can come back in a hurry if I need to. I'll bring a batch over to see you, maybe."

"Do," said Mr. Hamilton. "I like children. Poor things! I hope the trip to the country does them good."

Dick had read about fresh-air children who were much impressed by their first visit to the country, but this did not prepare him for the awed look on the faces of the twenty-five as they tumbled from the train at the little country depot, and made for the waiting stage.

"Now, children," said the matron, as Dick came up and introduced himself, "this is the gentleman who was so kind as to bring you out to this beautiful place," and she shook hands with the millionaire's son.

"Is dat de rich guy?" asked one boy, but though his words might sound disrespectful he did not intend them so.

"Hush!" exclaimed a girl in a much-patched red dress. "He'll hear you."

"What do I care! If I wuz as rich as him I wouldn't care who knowed it," retorted the boy.

"No more do I, old chap," replied Dick, with a laugh, as he patted the youngster on the back. "Now, boys and girls, the stage is waiting for you."

"Oh, Nellie!" cried a little tot with light hair, "we're goin' to ride in a real wagon with real horses!"

"Don't speak so loud!" was the whispered answer of her companion. "It's like a dream, an' maybe we'll wake up an' find it all gone."

The children, in spite of the fact that they came from the slums of New York, were all neat and clean, for that was one of the requirements of the committee that took charge of the fresh-air work. And, though their manners might be considered a little rough, they did not intend them so. It was due to the influence of their surroundings. Soon they had all piled into the stage, and the driver from Sunnyside started the four horses.

"Look, will yer! It's a regular tally-ho like de swells on Fif' Avenoo drives!" exclaimed the boy who had called Dick the "rich guy."

The ride to the farm was one continuous series of exclamations of delight from the boys and girls, who looked at the green fields on either side of the country road, at the comfortable farmhouses they passed, or at the range of mountains that towered off to the west.

"Look!" exclaimed one boy, who had kept tight hold of his sister's hand from the time he got off the train. "See, Maggie, that's where the sun goes to sleep. I never saw it before."

"Where?" asked the girl.

"Over there," and he pointed to the mountains behind which the golden orb was sinking to rest.

"Yes, dear," spoke the matron, who had overheard what was said, "and in the morning he'll get up and shine on the fields where you can run around and get strong.

"He's a sickly child," the matron added in a whisper to Dick. "I'm afraid he never will be strong. He has such queer fancies at times. His mother is a widow and goes out washing. The sister stays home and takes care of her little brother. It was a real charity that they could come, and I'm sure the committee doesn't know how to thank you for your generosity."

"Oh, pshaw! That's nothing," replied Dick, blushing like a girl at the praise. "I ought to do something with my money. I'm glad I heard about this fresh-air plan. I'll have some of the youngsters out next year if——"

Then he stopped. He happened to think that if his investments did not succeed he would not have much money to spend the next year, and, besides, he might be living with his Uncle Ezra at Dankville.

But the matron did not notice his hesitation, for, at that moment, the stage turned into the drive leading up to Sunnyside, and Dick was besieged by several inquiries.

"Say, mister, is dis a park?" asked one boy, as he saw the well-kept drive.

"No, this is the place where you are going to stay," Dick replied.

"Can we get out an' walk?" asked another, and this seemed to strike a popular chord, for that request became general. The matron nodded an assent and the children jumped out of the stage, some boys going by way of the windows.

"You can drive on and tell them we are coming," said Dick to the driver.

"Oh, I guess they'll know it fast enough," responded the man, with a grin. "You can hear them kids a mile."

Which was true enough, for the boys and girls were fairly yelling in pure delight. Dick and the matron walked on behind the crowd, the millionaire's son watching with interest the antics of the waifs.

"Johnny! Johnny!" yelled a slip of a girl to her bigger brother. "Come right off the grass this minute! Do youse want a cop to put you out? He don't know no better, mister," she said, turning to Dick. "He didn't mean nothin'. Johnny, do you hear me? Come off that grass right away, or the man will have youse arrested."

"No, no! Nothing of the sort!" exclaimed Dick, with a laugh. "You can eat the grass if you want to. Do just as you please. There isn't a policeman within twenty miles."

Then there was a mad rush over the big lawn that led up to Sunnyside. The children yelled, laughed, shouted, and fairly tumbled over each other in the very joy of being in the country. Pale cheeks reddened as the little lungs breathed in the pure, fresh air, dull eyes lighted up with pleasure, and little hands trembled with eagerness as they plucked buttercups, dandelions and daisies that grew on the far edges of the lawns.

"Wow!" yelled one lad. "Wow! I've got to do somethin' or I'll bust!"

And that is the way most of them felt it seemed, for they raced, ran, jumped and tumbled like children just let out after being kept in after school.

And such a supper as Mrs. Foster had provided for the waifs! Their eyes bulged as they came to the table that was fairly groaning under the weight of good things.

"Now," called Dick, when they sat down, "let me see how you can eat."

"They do not need any coaxing," replied the matron, and Dick soon saw that she was right.

That was only the beginning of a happy two weeks for the youngsters. They fairly went wild on the farm, for it had a hundred delights for them, from watching the cows being milked, to hunting for eggs in the big barn. Dick took them for automobile rides in relays, bringing several over to Hamilton Corners to see his father, who further delighted the childish hearts by gifts of dimes and nickels. On one of these trips the millionaire's son brought Tim Muldoon, the boy who had commented on Dick's riches that day the two met.

"An' does your governor own dat bank?" Tim asked, as Dick stopped the runabout in front of the institution.

"Well, most of it, I guess."

"An' can he go in dere an' git money whenever he wants it?"

"Yes, I guess he can."

"Say!" exclaimed Tim, as he looked weakly at Dick, "an youse is his son?"

"Yes."

"An' youse is takin' me an' dese (indicating some of the other youngsters) out fer a ride in dis gasolene gig? Us what ain't got a cent?"

"Yes; why not?" asked Dick, with a smile.

"Well, all I've got t' say is dat dis is as near bein' rich as I ever expects t' be, an' say, it's dead white of youse; dat's what it is. Why, dem rich guys in N' York would no more t'ink of treatin' us dis way dan dey would jump off de dock. Dat's straight!"

"Oh, I guess they would if they thought about it, but they probably don't know how many boys and girls would like to get out and see the country," said Dick, not wanting to take too much credit to himself.

"Like pie!" was Tim's contemptuous rejoinder. Then, as he was gazing rapturously at the entrance to the bank, he suddenly started as he saw a man coming down the steps.

"Say," he whispered to Dick, grabbing his arm, "is dat guy in your governor's bank?"

"Which man? What do you mean?"

"I mean dat one wid de black moustache, jest comin' down de steps. Is he in de bank?"

"Oh, that's Mr. Vanderhoof," replied Dick, recognizing the mining promoter.

"Mr. who?" asked Tim.

"Vanderhoof. Why, do you know him?"

"Not by dat name. But say, if he's got anyt'ing to do wit de bank it'll soon be on de blink."

"What do you mean?"

"I mean put out of business. On de blink, excuse my slang. But youse had better tell your governor to keep his peepers open."

"Why?" inquired Dick, a vague suspicion coming into his mind.

"Because," replied Tim, earnestly. "Dat man's name ain't Vanderhoof any more dan mine is."

"Who is he?"

"Why, he's William Jackson, or Bond Broker Bill. I seen him in de police court in N' York. I sells papers, an' I knows lots of de cops an' detectives. I saw 'em arrest dat man once, only he had a white beard an' moustache den. Now he's shaved off de whiskers an' colored his moustache, but I knowed him de minute I set me peepers on him. I seen his mug in de papers lots of times. Youse wants to be on lookout fer him or he'll put de bank on de blink. He's a gold-brick swindler, an' I guess up to any other woozy game he can make pay!"

"Bond Broker Bill! William Jackson! Colonel Dendon!" murmured Dick, in a daze. "No wonder I thought I had seen Mr. Vanderhoof before. It was in the New York hotel, where he tried to swindle me! And he sold dad and me some gold mining stock! I must tell dad right away!"

Dick looked after the retreating form of Mr. Vanderhoof. Then turning to Tim, who had made the startling disclosure, he said:

"Wait here for me! I must see my father at once," and getting out of the auto he hurried into the bank.

CHAPTER XXI

IN WHICH MR. VANDERHOOF VANISHES

Dick found his father busy, looking over some books and papers. He waited until the millionaire had finished and looked up, remarking:

"Well, Dick, what is it now? Some more of the fresh-air kids outside?"

"Yes, dad, but I've got something more important to tell you than about them. Was Mr. Vanderhoof just in here?"

"He was, and I took some more stock in the Hop Toad Mine. I had an additional report from the government assayer at Yazoo City, and the ore is richer than ever."

"You bought more stock, dad?"

"Yes. Why?"

"Because that man is a swindler! I just learned of it! His name is not Vanderhoof at all. He's the same man who tried to swindle me in New York. He goes by the name of Colonel Dendon. I thought there was something familiar about him the first day I saw him in here, but I couldn't place him on account of his dyed moustache. He's a swindler!"

"Who told you so?"

"Tim Muldoon, one of the fresh-air children. He saw him under arrest in New York. Probably he got out on bail. Oh, dad, I'm afraid we've both been swindled!"

"Well, don't get excited," counseled Mr. Hamilton, who was used to facing business troubles. "He may be a swindler, but I think our mining stock is good. The reports of it are all from reliable men. But I'll make an investigation at once."

"What will you do?"

"I think I'll send for Mr. Vanderhoof and ask him to explain. We'll have your friend Tim in here. No doubt it is all a mistake. I wouldn't place too much faith in what a boy says."

"You don't know Tim," responded Dick. "He's as bright as they make 'em. I guess all New York newsboys are. But where does Mr. Vanderhoof live?"

"He is stopping at the Globe Hotel. He told me he would remain in town about two weeks longer, as he had some business to transact. I'll just call up the hotel and ask him to come here. Meanwhile, tell Tim to come in."

"Don't 'phone, dad," advised Dick. "I'll run down to the hotel in my auto. If you call him on the wire he may suspect something. I'll bring him here in the machine."

"All right, Dick. Maybe that's a good plan. But don't get excited. Be calm. This may be only a boy's excited imagination. Mr. Vanderhoof certainly seemed like a business man and not like a swindler. Of course, I may be fooled. I have been, once or twice, in my time, but you've got to take those chances. However, we'll not decide anything until we talk to him. Go ahead."

"What will I do with the youngsters?" asked Dick. "I've got five of them with me."

"Give 'em a quarter apiece and let 'em buy ice-cream," advised the millionaire, with a laugh. "That is, all but Tim. Let him come in here and wait."

"Twenty-five cents' worth of ice-cream each would put them all in the hospital," explained Dick. "I'll make 'em distribute their wealth," and, in a few moments he had sent the four boys off to see the sights of the town, happy in the possession of a quarter of a dollar each, and with strict injunctions not to get lost, and to be back at the bank in an hour.

"Me to go inside de bank?" asked Tim, when Dick told him what was wanted. "Say, I'm gittin' real swell, I am! If de kids on Hester Street could see me now dey'd t'ink I was president of a railroad," and, with a laugh he went into Mr. Hamilton's private office. While Dick was gone the millionaire questioned the newsboy, who stuck to his story that the man he had seen was a swindler, who had been under arrest in New York.

Dick made fast time to the Globe Hotel. When he jumped from the auto, and hurried inside, the manager, who knew him, nodded a greeting.

"Is Mr. Vanderhoof about?" asked Dick, trying to keep his voice calm.

"Mr. Vanderhoof?" repeated the manager. "No, he went out a little while ago."

"Where?"

"Why, he said he was going back to New York," was the rather surprising answer. "A telegram came for him as soon as he got here and he left in a hurry. He just caught the express, and didn't even have time to take his baggage. He paid me his bill and rushed out in a hurry, telling me he'd send word where to forward his trunk. Did you want to see him about anything important?"

"It was, but I guess it will keep," replied Dick, trying not to show any alarm.

His worst fears were realized. Vanderhoof, *alias* Bond Broker Bill, had been warned by some confederates, perhaps, and had fled, after securing large sums of money from Dick and his father.

"And maybe we're not the only victims," thought Dick, as he left the hotel and turned the auto toward the bank.

"Well, what luck?" asked Mr. Hamilton, as his son entered.

"He's skipped out, dad!"

"He has, eh? Now to find out how badly we have been bitten. Dick, my boy, it looks as though there was a hoodoo hanging over your investments. Still, this mine stock may be all right. I'll wire to a lawyer in Yazoo City."

"Oh, he's a foxy guy, is Bond Broker Bill," said Tim, when Dick told him what had taken place. "I wish I'd a spotted him before. Maybe he seen me an' flew de coop."

"No, I don't believe he would have known you were on his trail," replied Dick, with an uneasy laugh. "I think he left on general principles."

It was several hours before Mr. Hamilton received a reply from the lawyer in Yazoo City, Nevada. When it came the telegram stated that the Hop Toad and Dolphin mines were producing a quantity of ore, and were generally believed to be good mines.

"Not much known about them here, though," the telegram went on. "Would advise a personal inspection. Believed that some promotor has a lot of stock and is trying to sell it in the East. Better look into it."

"Well, there's a chance yet," said Mr. Hamilton. "As I said, Vanderhoof may be a swindler, but the mines seem to be good. I'll have someone right on the ground look them up. We must make our plans carefully."

"Whom will you get, dad?"

"I don't know yet. I must write to this lawyer."

"Dad!" exclaimed Dick, suddenly. "Let me take a trip out West! Let me look up those mines! If they're no good I want to know it soon, so I can make some other investment. Can't I go to Nevada?"

CHAPTER XXII

OFF FOR THE WEST

Mr. Hamilton glanced at his son. Dick was all excited over the events of the last hour and by the sudden desire that had come to him.

"You go to Nevada?" repeated the millionaire.

"Yes, dad, and look up this mining business. I could see the lawyer and find out whether we have been swindled. The trip would do me good," he added, with a smile.

"I haven't any doubt of that, Dick," replied his father. "And, after thinking it over, I don't know but you could make whatever investigation would be needed. I think I'll let you go. How soon can you be ready?"

"To-night."

"Well, there's no such rush as that. If we've been swindled, finding it out now isn't going to help matters any. If, on the other hand, as I hope may be the case, the mines are all right, there's no need of hurrying out there. You'd better make good preparations for the trip. It isn't going to be much fun traveling alone."

"But, dad, I needn't travel alone. I was thinking I could take some of my chums with me. Bricktop, Frank Bender and Walter Mead would think it bully fun to go along. Why couldn't I take them?"

"I suppose you could if their parents did not object. They would be your guests, of course—that is, you would have to pay all expenses."

"I'd be willing to. I've got two thousand dollars invested in the Dolphin mine, and I've got to spend some more to see if I've thrown that money away. I might as well have some fun out of it, if I can."

"Four lads will make a nice party. I'll have McIverson go to the depot and get some time-tables. Meanwhile you had better get the fresh-air boys back to Sunnyside. It's getting near supper-time, and the matron may be worried about them."

"Say, is youse really goin' out where they make gold mines?" asked Tim Muldoon, as he and Dick went back to the automobile, around which the other lads, having spent all their money, and seen all the sights, were waiting. "Are youse goin' out West among de Indians an' cowboys?"

"Well, yes, but I guess there aren't any Indians left."

"Sure dere is! Didn't I read about in a book? It's a crackerjack! I'll lend it to youse. It's 'Three-Fingered Harry; or, De Scourge of de Redskins!'"

"No, thanks," answered Dick, with a laugh. "I wouldn't read such trash if I were you. There are very few Indians left out West and they're too scarce to kill off."

"Well," spoke Tim, with a sigh, "it's in de book. Say," he added, "does it cost much to go out West?"

"Well, I'm not sure just how much it does take, but I guess it's rather costly."

Tim sighed heavily.

"What's the matter?" asked Dick.

"I've got three dollars an' nineteen cents salted down in de dime savings bank," replied the newsboy. "I was savin' it fer a new overcoat, but I'd rather go out West. How far could I go fer three dollars an' nineteen cents? Could I travel wit youse as far as it lasted?"

The boy looked wistfully at Dick, and there was a world of longing in the blue eyes of Tim Muldoon as they met the brown orbs of the millionaire's son. Then Dick came to a sudden resolve.

"Would you like to go with me and the other boys?" he asked.

"Would I? Say, Mr. Dick, would a cat eat clams? Would I? Don't spring dat on me agin," he added, with an attempt at a laugh. "I've got a weak heart an' I might faint. It's back to little ole N' York an' Hester Street fer mine, I guess."

"No," said Dick. "I mean it. You may have rendered me and my father a great service, Tim, in telling us about Vanderhoof. If he proves to be what you say he is, a swindler, it is a good thing we found it out when we did. We may be able to save some of our money. If you can arrange to go I'll take you out West with me. Do you think you can?"

"Can I go? Well, I should say I can. Where's me ticket? I ain't got no trunk to pack."

"But what will your folks say?"

"I ain't got no folks, Mr. Dick. I'm all dere is," and, though he spoke flippantly, there was a suspicion of tears in Tim's eyes.

"Then, if the matron who brought you here says it is all right, you shall go," decided Dick.

Dick was actuated by two motives. He wanted to give pleasure to the little waif, to whom he had taken a great liking, and he also felt that Tim might be of service to him. If Vanderhoof turned up out in Nevada, it might be well to have Tim on hand to confront him. Then, too, Tim was a bright, quick lad, and Dick felt he would be useful on the trip.

Dick returned his charges to Sunnyside, and the matron, after hearing of the plans for the western trip, readily consented that Tim should go. He was an orphan, she explained, who had been taken in charge by a philanthropic society in New York. The boy was good-hearted and honest, she said, and had proved that he could be trusted. While his talk might be a bit rough and slangy a true heart beat under Tim's patched but neat jacket.

In spite of the prospective trip Dick did not forget the fresh-air children. It was found that it would require several days to get the through tickets for Yazoo City, and, in the meanwhile, the millionaire's son arranged for a big outdoor clambake for the youngsters. He and the three boys, whom he had invited to make the long journey with him, attended, and helped the waifs to have a good time—if they needed such assistance, which was doubtful.

Then, after arranging for another lot of the little unfortunates to come to Sunnyside when the first crowd had reached New York, Dick bade good-bye to those into whose lives he had been able to bring much happiness because of his wealth.

Tim was taken to the Hamilton mansion, where he was fitted up in a manner that made him think he had fallen heir to some vast treasure, such as those he read about in dime novels.

"If me Hester Street friends could see me now," he murmured, as he looked at the new suit Dick had bought him, "dey would sure take me for a swell."

"Don't think too much of good clothes," warned Dick.

"Well, it's de first time I ever had any to t'ink about," replied Tim, "an' youse must let me look at dem till I gits used to 'em," which Dick laughingly agreed to do.

"I hear you're going out West," remarked Henry Darby to Dick, when he met him on the street the day before that set for the start.

"Yes. Going to look up some gold mines," and Dick laughed.

"If you find any lying around loose, or one that no one else wants—or even an old one that someone has thrown away—why just express it back to me," requested Henry. "I'd rather have a good gold mine than this old metal business, I think."

"How is it going?" asked Dick.

"Pretty well. Say, I don't think I ought to keep that hundred-dollar check you sent me for telling you that I'd seen Grit in the man's wagon."

"Of course you've got to keep it!" exclaimed Dick. "I would have paid it to the first person who gave me the right clue, and I'm sure I couldn't give it to anyone I like better than you."

"It certainly came in mighty handy," said Henry.

"Why?"

"I had a chance to buy up the refuse from an old boiler factory just before I got it and I hadn't any cash. Dad had taken all the surplus. He's got some scheme on hand, and he won't tell me what it is. He says there's lots of money in it. There may be," went on Henry, with an odd smile, "but what's worrying me is whether dad is going to get the money out of it. That's mostly the trouble with his schemes. There's thousands of dollars in 'em, but the cash generally stays there for all of him. But maybe this one will turn out all right. I hope so, because he's got all the surplus. But I used the hundred dollars to buy some old iron, and I think I can dispose of it at a profit. Well, I hope you have good luck."

"Thanks," answered Dick. "I'll remember what you said about a gold mine."

"Well, I'll not insist on a gold mine," called back Henry, as he started his horse up, a task that required some time, for the animal seemed to take advantage of every stop to go to sleep. "I'm not prejudiced in favor of a gold mine. A good-paying silver mine will do pretty nearly as well."

"I'll remember, Henry. Good-bye until I get back."

Early the next morning Dick and his four boy friends were on their way to the West. Their train was an express and the first stop was at a large city, where several railroads formed a junction. As the boys were looking from the window of the parlor car, Tim, who managed to take his eyes away from the gorgeous fittings long enough to notice what was going on up and down the long station platform, suddenly uttered an exclamation, and grabbed Dick's arm.

"Look! Dere he is!" he whispered.

"Who?"

"Vanderhoof! Colonel Dendon! Bond Broker Bill!"

"Where? I don't see anyone."

"Dat slick-lookin' man, wid de brown hat on," and Tim pointed to him.

"But he hasn't any black moustache," objected Dick, thinking Tim's imagination was getting the best of him.

"Of course not. He's cut it off. But I'd know him anywhere by dat scar on his left cheek. Dat's de swindler all right!"

As Dick looked he saw that the man with the brown hat did have a large scar on his cheek. It had been hidden by the moustache before.

Then, just as the train pulled out, the man looked toward the parlor car. His eyes met Dick's, and, an instant later, the man with the scar was on the run toward the telegraph office.

CHAPTER XXIII

AT THE MINES

"Hold on!" cried Dick, jumping up. "Stop the train!"

The cars were rapidly acquiring speed, and Dick ran toward the door with the evident intention of getting off.

"Don't jump, Dick!" called Walter Mead. "We're going too fast!"

"Dat's right," chimed in Tim. "It's too late!"

"Yes, I guess it is," assented Dick. "But, Tim, how do you know that was Vanderhoof? To me he didn't look a bit like him. Besides, how did you know he had a scar under his moustache?"

"I've seen him wid his whiskers an' moustache off before," replied the newsboy. "I used to run errands for de sleuths at police headquarters, an' I seen lots of criminals."

"But are you sure you saw this man there?"

"Cert. He was brought in lots of times fer some kind of crooked game, but most times he was let go, 'cause they couldn't prove anyt'ing agin him. Sometimes he'd have a white beard an' agin a black moustache, but dem fly cops, dem gum-shoe sleuths, dey knowed him every time. I'll stake me reputation dat was him on de platform."

"But what can he be doing here?" asked Dick, "and why should he make a bee-line for the telegraph office when he saw me? I'm positive he knew who I was."

"Course he did," replied Tim. "He's probably sendin' a telegram to some of his friends in Yazoo City t' be on de lookout for youse."

"Do you think so? But how would he know I had started for there?"

"Say," inquired Tim, in drawling tones, "don't de hull town where you live know dat Millionaire Hamilton's son is goin' off on a journey in a palace car, an' takin' some friends, includin' Tim Muldoon, wid him? In course dey does. An' youse can bet your bottom dollar dat everybody in Hamilton Corners is talkin' about it. Vanderhoof, or Bond Broker Bill, knowed it as soon as anybody, an' if he's been puttin' up a crooked deal he's gittin' ready t' fix t'ings on de other end—at Yazoo City, I mean."

"Then, if he has warned his confederates out West," went on Dick, "there's not much use in my going there to make an investigation. They'd be sure to have things fixed up to deceive me. I depended on finding out about the mines before those in charge knew who I was."

"You can do dat yet," said Tim.

"How?"

"Why, lay low, dat's how. Don't go out dere wid de idea of handin' your visitin' card t' every guy you meet. Drift int' town easy like an' look about on de quiet fer a few days. Den youse kin see how de land lays an' git a line on de fakers. After dat youse can go up to de villain like de hero does in de play an' say: 'Now den, Red-Handed Mike, I have caught youse at last! You shall give me dose paper-r-r-r-s er I'll shoot you down like a dog!'" and Tim laughed with the others at his imitation of the methods of the actors on the stage when a cheap melodrama is being performed.

"I don't know but your advice is good," agreed Dick. "I can't catch Vanderhoof now, but perhaps we can spoil his plans. Let's have a consultation and decide what's best to do."

The boys had the parlor car pretty much to themselves, and their talk was not likely to be overheard by the other passengers who were in the farther end.

The journey was a pleasant one, and the boys enjoyed every hour of it. The country through which they passed presented, almost constantly, something new in the way of scenery, and as they proceeded farther and farther west the boys were wild with delight at the beautiful prospect, the wild stretches of country and the glimpses of the free life on the plains.

Sleeping in the berths, eating in the dining-car and looking out of the windows of the big Pullman were keen delights to Dick's companions, none of whom had ever traveled in such a fashion before, though to the millionaire's son it was more or less familiar.

When they reached the last stage of their journey and were within a few hours' ride of Yazoo City the five boys, at Tim's suggestion, changed from the parlor car to an ordinary one.

"It'll look better t' climb down out of a poor man's car dan from de coach wid de velvet curtains at de windows," he said. "Students ain't supposed t' be lookin' fer places t' t'row money away." For they had agreed to pass themselves off as students, come West to look at mines in general.

Thus it was that no unusual comments were made by the crowd at the station in Yazoo City when the five boys and a few other passengers alighted from the train.

It was a typical Western town, rather larger than an ordinary one, for it was the centre for a prosperous mining section. Across from the station were two hotels, one called the Imperial Inn and the other the Royal Hotel.

"Doesn't seem to be much choice," observed Frank Bender. "Neither one looks as if royalty was in the habit of stopping at it."

"We'll go to the Royal," decided Dick. "The lawyer, whom dad wrote to about the mine, stops there, and I want to see him."

Accordingly the five boys walked across the street and entered the lobby of the hotel. It was even less pretentious on the inside than viewed from without, but it looked clean. Dick led the way up to the desk, to engage rooms for himself and friends.

"Glad t' see you, strangers," greeted the man behind the desk with easy familiarity. "What might yo' uns be, if I might make so bold as to ask? Travelin' show or capitalists lookin' fer a good payin' mine?"

"We're studying mining conditions," replied Dick. "Traveling for information."

"Ah, I see," interrupted the hotel proprietor, who also acted as clerk. "We've had some of you college boys out here before. Welcome to Yazoo City," and Dick and his companions were glad that the man had put his own interpretation on their object in coming West. He swung the book around to them and Dick signed first. The pen was poor and the ink worse, so it was no wonder that his name, when he had scratched it down, looked like anything but Dick Hamilton. Nor did the others do any better.

They were shown to their rooms, and, as it was late afternoon, they decided to defer beginning their investigations until the next day. The supper was good but plain, though the boys were more interested in watching the men about them, and hearing them talk, than they were in eating, hungry as they were.

They slept soundly, though Dick was awakened once or twice by revolver shots and loud yelling. He thought someone had been hurt, but on inquiring from a porter, passing through the hall, learned that he need have no cause for alarm.

"Land love yo', son!" said the porter, a burly Westerner. "Them's only th' boys gittin' rid of some of their animal spirits. Don't worry none. They seldom shoots this way, an' if they does they aims high, so they only busts the top window lights. Yo' ain't got nothin' t' be askeered of."

But though Dick was not exactly easy in his mind his rest was not disturbed by any bullets coming through his window, though there was considerable shooting all night.

"I think we'll take a trip out to the mines right after breakfast," decided Dick, when the boys had gathered in his room after dressing. "I'll hire a big carriage and we can all go. I inquired about them, and I learned that the Dolphin and Hop Toad mines are close together, a few miles outside of town."

"I think I'll stay around here," decided Tim.

"Why?" asked Dick.

"Because I want to see if anyt'ing happens. Youse kin go out to de holes in de ground. I'll see 'em later if dere worth lookin' at. But I t'ink I'll mosey around de hotel a while."

"Well, maybe it will be a good plan," agreed Dick. "We can't tell what sort of a game Vanderhoof is up to. Now, come on down to breakfast, boys."

After the meal Dick hired a large three-seated buckboard, and he and his chums were driven off toward the mines. The news had quickly gone around that they were young college students, who had come West to get practical illustrations bearing on their studies.

Tim stood on the hotel steps looking after Dick and his chums. As the carriage disappeared around a turn in the road someone came up to the newsboy and tapped him on the shoulder. He turned quickly and saw, standing beside him, a well-dressed lad about his own age. The youth wore a showy watch chain and assumed a confident air that was not at all in keeping with his years.

"How's my friend, Dick Hamilton?" he asked, nodding in the direction of the carriage.

"Dick Hamilton," spoke Tim, in a sort of daze.

"Yes, Dick Hamilton, of Hamilton Corners. I suppose he came out here to see about the mines he and his millionaire father invested in."

"Mines," repeated Tim, somewhat surprised to thus learn that Dick's object was already discovered.

"Yes, mines," went on the other youth. "Oh, I know all about it. Dick thought he was cute, pretending to come here with a bunch of college lads. But I'm on to him, and so are the others."

"Who are you?" asked Tim, boldly.

"Just tell Dick that Simon Scardale was asking for him," replied the flashily-dressed youth, as he moved away. "I'll not give him my address, because I don't believe he'd like to call on me, but just tell him Simon Scardale was asking for him," and, with a mocking bow, Simon jumped on a pony and galloped off down the street.

CHAPTER XXIV

A NIGHT TRIP

Dick and his chums saw many interesting sights on their drive to the mines. All about them were evidences of the hustling West, and the noise of the stamping mills, or machines, which crush up the rocks and ore to enable the precious metals to be extracted from them could be heard on every side. They met many teams hauling ore from the mines to distant "stamps," and saw throngs of miners in their rough, but picturesque, garb, tramping along.

"Do you think they'll let us visit the mines?" asked Dick of the driver. "We want to find out all we can about 'em."

"Oh, I guess so. This is a free and easy country. Visitors are always welcome, providin' they don't want to know too much," and the driver winked his eye.

"Too much?" repeated Dick.

"Yes. Lots of men out here don't care to have their past history raked over. It ain't always healthy, son, to ask a man where he came from, or why he left there. There's secrets, you understand, that a man don't like strangers to know."

"I understand," replied Dick, with a laugh. "But we only want to see how they get the gold out of mines."

"Oh, yes, you can see that," was the driver's answer. "But there's lots of mines nearer than the Hop Toad and the Dolphin; lots of 'em."

"Aren't those good mines?" asked Dick, anxious to get the opinion of what might be presumed to be an unprejudiced observer.

"Well, so folks say," was the cautious answer. "All mines is good—until they're found out to be bad. I guess they're getting gold out of both mines. Leastways, that's what the men that's working 'em say."

When the buckboard with its passengers arrived at the Hop Toad mine the driver called to a man who seemed to be in charge:

"Say, Nick, here's a crowd of college students that want to see how you make gold. Any objections?"

The man addressed looked up quickly. Dick knew at once, from a description the lawyer had sent to Mr. Hamilton, that the man was Nick Smith, commonly known as "Forty-niner Smith," an old-time miner, who was in charge of the active operations at the two mines Dick and his father were interested in. But Dick resolved not to disclose his own identity unless it became necessary to do so.

"Come on, and welcome," responded Forty-niner Smith, with an assumed heartiness, but Dick did not like the look on the man's face. "We're just settin' off a blast," the miner went on. "Th' tenderfeet kin see a bucket full of gold in a minute."

The boys joined a group of waiting miners, who regarded them curiously. All about were piles of ore and, not far away, were the ruins of a stamp-mill.

"Our stamp's out of business," said Smith, noting Dick's glance at it. "We send our ore, and that from the Dolphin, down to the Wild Tiger mill. They're crushing it for us. Ah, boys, there she goes!"

There was a dull rumble from a hole in the ground, and the earth seemed to tremble. Then some smoke lazily floated from the mouth of the mine.

"As soon as it clears away they'll send up some gold ore," went on Smith, and, in a short time, a big iron bucket came to the surface on a strong, wire cable. It was filled with what looked like pieces of stone, but Smith, taking some of the fragments, passed them to Dick.

"See that yellow stuff!" he exclaimed, pointing to numerous shining particles. "That's pure gold! Here, take some samples along," he added, in a burst of generosity. "We'll never miss 'em," and he filled the hands of the four boys with the precious metal. "This is one of the richest mines in this locality," he added. "Now come on over and I'll show you the Dolphin," and he led the way toward the ruins of the stamp-mill.

"Somebody dropped a dynamite cartridge near it," he explained as he passed it. "But we don't mind. We've ordered two new ones. I guess they've got through blasting here. Yes, here comes some ore," he went on as a bucket of the stuff that looked like broken cobblestones came to the surface.

Dick's heart beat fast. At last he was looking at the mine in which he had invested two thousand dollars. And, best of all, real gold was being taken from it. At least it looked like real gold, and had the same appearance as that from the Hop Toad mine. Besides, if it was not gold, why would the men work so hard to get it up?

"Maybe I'm having all my trouble for my pains," thought Dick. "I guess these mines are good, after all. Vanderhoof may have been a swindler, but this looks as if dad and I had made good investments."

"Here, have some of this ore," added Smith, with another show of generosity. "We'll never miss it. Have it made into watch charms or scarf pins. That's what lots of 'em do."

"Can we go down in the mine?" asked Frank Bender.

"Not to-day," replied Smith, with a sharp look at Dick. "You see it's a little dangerous, so soon after a blast, unless you've had some experience. Come out some other day and maybe you can. Glad to see visitors any time. Now, if you'll excuse me, I'll have to go and see about sending some of this ore to the stamp-mill. It's so rich we have to send a guard with it to protect it from thieves," he added, in a burst of confidence.

"Well, I guess we've seen enough," spoke Dick. "Come on, boys."

As they rode back to the hotel, Dick soon decided on a plan of action. He would take to a government assayer the ore he and his companions had received, and learn whether the mine was or was not a good one. This time there would be no chance for deception, he thought. He had seen, with his own eyes, the ore taken from the mine. The government assayer, he knew, would tell the truth about the value of it. Then he could be satisfied that his investment, as well as his father's, was a good one.

Explaining his purpose to the boys they readily gave Dick their samples of ore, though he suggested they save small pieces for souvenirs, which they did.

"Maybe you'd better see the lawyer your father wrote to," suggested Walter Mead, when they were almost at the hotel.

"Good idea," declared Dick, but he could not carry it out, for, on inquiring, he learned that the lawyer had gone on a journey and would not be back for a month.

"I'll go ahead on my own responsibility," Dick decided. "I think I'll hunt up the government assayer. I wonder where Tim is?"

The newsboy was not about the hotel, and, thinking he had gone off to see the sights, Dick did not look for him. He got the address of the assayer from the hotel proprietor, and was soon at the official's office.

"So you want some of this Hop Toad, and Dolphin ore tested, eh?" inquired the assayer. "Well, you're not the first person who has brought me some. I tested some for a man named Hamilton, away out East, some time ago. His lawyer brought it to me. I found it good then and I guess it's good yet."

"Was it really good?" asked Dick, eagerly, and then, judging the government official could be trusted, he told the object of his western trip.

"Young man," said the assayer, when Dick had finished, "I'll tell you all I know. This ore is good. It's very rich. In fact, I don't need to assay it to tell that it runs many dollars to the ton. But one thing I can't tell you to a certainty is that it came from the Hop Toad or Dolphin mine. You see we assayers have to take the word of the miners as to where the ore comes from. All we do is to make a test, and, by finding out how much gold there is to a certain amount of ore, figure out how much it will assay to a ton of the same ore. That's the basis on which mines are valued."

"I can assure you that this ore we have came from the Dolphin and Hop Toad mines," said Dick. "We saw it taken out."

"Seeing isn't always believing, when it comes to mines," replied the assayer. "Still it may have been taken directly from the drifts. I wouldn't say it to everyone," he went on, "but I believe there is something crooked about those mines. I have thought so for some time, but I can't decide just what it is. They have a reputation of being very rich, and the ore assays well, but I don't like the actions of the men running them."

"Do you think I have been cheated?" asked Dick.

"I do, but I can't give my reasons for it."

"Then what would you advise?"

"Well, you're out here to investigate. Keep on investigating. I'm a government official and I can't take either side. But if I were you," and he came close to Dick and spoke in a low tone, "I'd visit that mine when none of the men were around. I think they knew you were coming and prepared for you."

"Why?" asked Dick, much surprised.

"Well, I can't tell you all my reasons now. Do as I advise, and try to inspect the mines when no one is around."

"When would be the best time for that?"

"At night. That's the only time it would be safe. But be very careful. This is a queer country. Men act quickly out here and they don't always stop to ask questions before they shoot. But you boys are quick and sharp and— well, good luck to you, that's all I can say."

"I'm much obliged to you," answered Dick. "I'll do as you advise."

As he and his chums left the assayer's office they met Tim, who had returned to the hotel, and, on inquiring, had learned where they had gone.

"Have a good time?" asked Dick, of his newsboy friend.

"Not so very," replied Tim, rather solemnly.

"Why not?"

"Because I was chasin' after a fellow what called himself Simon Scardale, and I couldn't catch him."

"Simon Scardale here?" exclaimed Dick.

"That's what he is, and he's on to our game," replied Tim. "Dick, youse has got to act quick, I guess."

For a few moments Dick was too surprised to know what to say. He began to see through it now. Simon was a friend of Vanderhoof, and, though he might not be mixed up in the swindling games, he had, likely, given information that would prevent the millionaire's son from accomplishing his object. Dick was in a maze. He was not altogether sure that the mines were a swindle, but he strongly suspected it. Simon's presence in the western city seemed to argue that some strange game was about to be played.

"We must talk this over," decided Dick. "Come on, boys. We'll go back to the hotel and have a conference. Then we can decide what to do."

In Dick's room the chums went over all the points of the matter. But, try as they did, they could not see a reason for Simon's presence in Yazoo City, nor for his remarks to Tim.

"But dat government feller give youse good advice," declared the newsboy. "Why don't youse go out to de mine? Maybe youse kin git on to der game. I'm wid youse."

"I believe I will," decided Dick. "Tim, you and Frank and I will go. Yes, Walter, you and Bricktop had better stay at the hotel," he added, as he saw a look of disappointment come over the faces of the other two boys. "Five would be too many, and, by some of us staying here, there will be less liability of suspicion. We'll make a night trip to the mine and, if it's at all possible, I'll go down inside."

"Dat's de way to talk!" exclaimed Tim.

Cautiously they made their plans. Dick decided he and his two companions would walk to the mines, as, if they hired a rig, it would become known to Smith or Simon, who were probably spying on their actions. Tim related how he had tried to follow Simon when he rode off on the pony, but had been unsuccessful.

"It's a nice moonlight night," said Dick, when the plans had been made. "We can take some candles with us and I guess we can get down the cable at the mine. Then we'll see if there's any crooked work going on."

After supper Tim, Frank and Dick started off. They little realized what was before them, or perhaps they would not have been so light-hearted.

CHAPTER XXV

DOWN IN A GOLD MINE

"It's going to take over two hours to get out there," said Dick, as he and his companions tramped on. "I don't know how long we'll stay. It all depends on circumstances. If they discover us we'll not stay as long as we otherwise would," and he laughed. "But I guess it's an all-night job. Well, the road is a good one, and it's a nice night."

"That's what it is," answered Frank. "That moon looks as if it was pure silver, hung up there in the sky."

"You're getting poetical," commented Dick.

"Dat oughter be a gold moon to be right in de swim," was Tim's opinion.

"What do you expect to do when you get to the mine?" asked Frank, as, now that they were beyond the borders of Yazoo City, they were not afraid to talk of their object.

"I hardly know," answered Dick. "What I want to find out is whether or not that mine is a fake one."

"How do youse tell a fake gold mine?" asked Tim. "Is it like a lead nickel or counterfeit money so youse can tell by bitin' a chunk of it?"

"Hardly," replied Dick, with a laugh. "I've been reading up about mines lately, and, according to the book, the most common way of making a fake mine is to 'salt' it, or 'sweat' it."

"Salt it?" repeated Frank. "I've heard of salting cattle, but never mines."

"That doesn't describe it very well," went on Dick, "but that's what they call it. Sometimes it is termed 'sweating.' By either way it means making the ore in the mine look as if it was filled with gold, when, in fact, the gold had only been put there by some man who wanted a worthless mine to look like a good one."

"How do they do it?" asked Tim.

"The most common way is to take some real gold dust, put it into a shotgun, load it heavily with powder and shoot it at the side of the mine. The gold particles are shot into the rock a little way and it appears like real ore. They do this several times down the sides of a rocky mine and it looks very much like the real thing. After a man has bought the mine and begins to dig, he discovers it's all a fake."

"Wow!" exclaimed Tim. "T'ink of shootin' gold out of a gun. I wish somebody'd take a few shots at me. Easy ones, of course, so's I could live to enjoy it."

"There are other ways of making fake mines," went on Dick, "but I didn't read much about them."

"Do you think the Hop Toad and Dolphin mines are fakes?" asked Frank.

"That's what I'm afraid of. But I'm pretty sure Smith and his confederates didn't use any such method as shooting the gold into the rocks. It's in too deep for that, and they could hardly hope to fool the assayer that way. No, they must have some new scheme, and maybe I can discover it."

The boys walked along briskly, and, almost before they realized it, they saw that they were approaching the mine.

"Now, go easy," advised Dick. "We first want to see if there is anyone in sight. If not, we'll take a trip down."

Near the mouth of the shaft was some machinery used to lift the bucket from the mine. The boys could see the dull gleam of the coals under the boiler of the hoisting apparatus, for the fire had been banked. But there was no sign of anyone around, and, after peering cautiously about, the boys reached the edge of the shaft.

"Now, if dey had an elevator fer us it would be dead easy," spoke Tim. "But I don't see how youse is goin' to git down."

"Wait until I take a look," replied Dick.

He approached the mouth of the mine and uttered an exclamation that brought the other boys to his side.

"There's a ladder leading down," he said. "We can use that. Now to explore a gold mine."

Seeing that he had his candles and matches ready, Dick began to descend. The other boys waited until he was down some distance and then followed. The ladder, as they could see, was built against the side of the shaft, and it was far enough away so that the ascending or descending bucket did not touch it.

"Hold on!" cried Dick, from the dark depths. "I'm going to light a candle."

Presently a faint gleam came up the shaft, and Tim and Frank could make out Dick's form standing below them on a rung of the ladder. They also lighted candles, and the descent continued. In about a minute Dick called again:

"Easy now, fellows; I've struck bottom. Got down to the first level, I guess."

In a little while Tim and Frank joined him. They found they were standing in a sort of cave, hollowed out under ground. Resting at the foot of the shaft was a big bucket, attached to the wire cable that extended to the hoisting drum.

"Is dis all dere is to de mine?" asked Tim.

"No, there seems to be a gallery leading off to no one knows where," replied Dick, pointing to a gloomy hole. "Come on, boys, I haven't seen any gold yet," and he waved his candle to and fro. It flickered over the rocky walls of the mine. They glistened with water that oozed from many crevices, but there was no glitter of the precious metal.

The boys walked cautiously along the gallery, or tunnel, that extended at right angles to the perpendicular shaft. Suddenly, Dick, who was in the lead, stopped short.

"Hush!" he exclaimed, in a whisper. "I hear voices."

The boys listened. From somewhere in the darkness ahead of them came an indistinct murmur.

"Come ahead, easy!" whispered the millionaire's son.

They advanced on tiptoes. The murmur of voices became louder. Then, as the boys made a turn in the tunnel, a strange scene was suddenly presented to them.

In a sort of cave, formed by the widening of the gallery, a number of men stood in a group. Several torches, stuck into cracks in the rocky wall, gave light. But, strangest of all, was the occupation of the men.

One of them was stirring what seemed like a mass of mortar in a wooden box, such as masons use. Into it another was pouring from a sack, gleaming, golden, yellow particles, which, as the light gleamed on them, glittered like gold.

"Seems like throwing the yellow stuff away," remarked the man who held the sack.

"What of it. We'll get it back five times over," replied the one who, with a hoe, was stirring the stuff. "It's like planting gold in a garden. It grows, you know. This mine is our garden."

"They're 'salting' the mine," whispered Dick to his companions.

Off to one side another man was drilling holes in the soft rock. The musical clink of his hammer on the drill sounded faint and far off, so muffled was it.

"Haven't you got that stuff ready yet?" called the man with the drill. "I've got all the holes bored. Hurry up and get it in or it won't be hard by to-morrow, and there's no telling when that Hamilton kid may take a notion to drop in and visit his mine," and he laughed.

"Oh, I guess I can keep him away for a few days yet," answered one, whom Dick recognized as Forty-niner Smith. "I've got a game I haven't played. But I guess this stuff is mixed enough. Say, it's the best scheme I've struck yet for 'sweating' a mine. Beats the shotguns all to pieces."

From their hiding place the boys watched what the men did. The mixture with the gold particles in it was poured into the holes the man had dug. The boys could see now that it was not mortar, but concrete, which was being used. To Dick the whole scheme was now plain.

The men poured a lot of gold dust into some concrete, and mixed it up with water until it was about as thick as paste. Then they put it into holes drilled in the rocky walls of the mine. The concrete hardened and became almost like the rock itself. Then, when a blast was set off, the rock, concrete and gold was all blown into small pieces, so that it looked as if the ore was of good, gold-bearing quality, whereas it was nothing but ordinary rock "salted."

That was how the men were working to fool investors. They had taken an abandoned mine, from which all the gold had been dug, and, by this ingenious method, made it look, to the ignorant, as though it was a regular bonanza.

"Well," remarked Dick, in a whisper, "we've discovered the trick. I guess dad's money and mine, too, is 'gone up the flume,' as the miners say. But I'm glad——"

At that moment, Frank, who was balancing himself on a bit of rock, in order to see better, stumbled and fell, making quite a noise. The men turned as if a shot had been fired.

"What's that?" asked Smith, in a hoarse whisper.

"Some loose rock caving in," answered one of the men. "Come on, finish up. We've only got one more hole to fill, and by that time Nash will be ready to hoist us up."

"That wasn't falling rock!" declared Smith. "Boys, I believe someone is spying on us. I'm going to take a look."

Seizing one of the torches he started toward where Dick and his companions were hiding.

"Come on!" exclaimed the millionaire's son, pulling Tim and Frank by the arm. "We've got to get out of this!"

They turned and ran, their footsteps echoing on the rocky floor of the mine. They could hear Smith coming after them. His torch flashed around the turn in the gallery. He caught sight of them.

"Stop!" he cried. "Stop or I'll shoot!"

CHAPTER XXVI

SIMON'S CONFESSION

Dick gave a hurried look behind him. He could see something shining in Smith's hand—something that the light from the torch glinted on.

"Keep on!" hoarsely whispered Tim. "He can't hit us down here. Keep on!"

Stumbling, almost falling, their candles showing but faint blue points of light as the flame flickered away from the wicks because of their speed, the boys ran toward the bottom of the shaft.

"If we reach the ladder I think we can get away," said Frank, panting from his exertion.

It seemed as if it was a mile back to the shaft, but it was only a few hundred feet. The boys expected every minute to hear the shot ring out. They caught the sounds of the footfalls of their pursuer and they sounded nearer and nearer. He was familiar with the gallery and his torch gave him better light to go by than did the candles give the boys.

Once more the angry miner's voice called:

"Hold on, whoever you are, or I'll shoot!"

"Quick! There's the shaft!" exclaimed Dick, pointing to where the big bucket rested at the bottom of the opening.

The boys made a rush for it. At the same instant a shot rang out in the darkness, the flash from the revolver lighting up the mine cavern with sudden glare. They could hear the bullet strike far above their heads with a vicious "ping!" Clearly, Smith was only firing to scare them, and did not want to run any chances of hurting them, as he had aimed high.

Then a strange thing happened. The cable, attached to the bucket, began to wind upward. There was considerable slack to it and the bucket did not immediately follow. It was evident that the machinery at the shaft mouth had started and that the ore-carrier was about to be hoisted up. An inspiration came to Dick.

"Into the bucket!" he called. "It's big enough to hold us all and we'll be hauled to the top! We can escape that way!"

Tim and Frank needed no further urging. They clambered over the iron sides of the bucket, followed by Dick. And not a second too soon, for, as he set his feet on the iron bottom, the cable tauted and the bucket started upward.

"Come back here!" yelled Smith, reaching the bottom of the shaft just in time to see the conveyor disappearing. He made an ineffectual grab for it, but, as his torch flared up when he threw it on the ground, the better to use his hands, Dick, looking over the edge of the iron receptacle, saw that the ugly miner was fifteen feet below them.

"Pull your head in!" advised Frank. "He might shoot!"

But Smith had no such intentions. Making a sort of megaphone of his hands, he shouted up the shaft:

"Nash! Nash! Stop the engine! Don't hoist the bucket! We're not in it!"

But the engineer at the mouth of the shaft never heard him. Higher and higher went the bucket, carrying the boys. They looked up the black opening and could see the moon shining overhead.

"Lucky escape!" murmured Dick. "I wonder how that bucket came to go up just when we needed it most?"

He learned a minute later. As the conveyor reached the surface and stopped, Dick and his friends stepped out. They saw that the fire under the boiler was burning brightly, and that a man, who had not been there when they arrived, was attending to the hoisting engine. As he caught sight of them he exclaimed:

"Who are you? Where's Smith?"

"Down there," replied Dick, not caring to go into details. "Come on, boys."

"But something's wrong," went on Nash, the engineer. "I was told to come here about one o'clock, get up steam and be ready to hoist the bucket when I heard a revolver shot. I heard it and I hoisted away. But where's Smith and his men? He told me he'd fire a shot when he was ready to come up. I heard it plain enough, but who are you?"

"Smith will explain," replied Dick. "We came up first, that's all," he added, coolly. "Come on, boys."

Leaving behind them a much-puzzled engineer, the three boys hurried away from the mine. They were soon on the road leading back to Yazoo City.

"Do you think they'll chase us?" asked Frank.

"I don't believe so," replied Dick. "I guess Smith is worried enough as it is. He may suspect who we were, but I don't believe he knows for certain. However, we'll keep in the shadows for a way."

This they did, but there was no need of apprehension, for none of the miners pursued them.

"Well, youse had your money's worth of excitement, anyway," commented Tim. "Say, I t'ought it was all up wid me dere, one spell. But youse had your nerve wid you, Mr. Dick."

"Well, we had some luck with us, too," replied the millionaire's son. "Those fellows played right into our hands. They must have gone down the mine early in the evening, and arranged with the engineer to come back, when they were finished with their 'salting' process, to hoist up their tools and things so as to leave nothing suspicious around. When Smith fired at us the engineer, who arrived after we had gone down the mine, thought it was the signal agreed upon and he hoisted away. I guess he was surprised when he saw us get out of the bucket."

"And I guess Smith will be surprised when he finds out you know how he and his gang fixed up the fake mine," remarked Frank.

"I guess the best plan will be to say nothing to him about it," said Dick. "I don't see anything for me to do but go back home and report to dad. We've been swindled, and I'm out two thousand dollars. I don't know how much he lost. The Hop Toad and Dolphin mines aren't worth anything, I'm afraid."

"Did youse lose two t'ousand dollars?" asked Tim, as the boys hurried along the moonlit road.

"I'm afraid so."

"An' youse ain't agoin' to faint over it? Say, youse has got nerve, youse has," added the newsboy, admiringly. "Youse oughter be in N' York. How'd you come to put so much money in a fake mine?"

"I didn't know it was a fake," replied the wealthy youth.

The boys reached their hotel in the gray dawn of the early morning. They were worn out and tired from their long tramp and the excitement of the night. As they entered the lobby, where a sleepy clerk was on duty behind the desk, the latter called to them:

"I say, is one of you named Dick Hamilton?"

"I am," replied the millionaire's son.

"Well, I've got a message for you from a lad named Simon Scardale."

"Simon Scardale?" repeated Dick.

"Yes. He was badly hurt last night by a fall from a horse he was riding. He's over at the other hotel, and he sent word that he wanted to see Dick Hamilton as soon as he came in. I looked over the register, but I couldn't see anyone by that name, and I thought he'd made a mistake."

Dick recalled his scrawling signature on the book, and did not wonder that the clerk could not make it out.

Telling Tim and Frank to go upstairs and notify Bricktop and Walter of their safe arrival, Dick started for the Imperial Inn. He found the night clerk on duty, and, telling his object, was shown upstairs by a sleepy bell-boy.

As he entered the room he saw Simon in bed. The youth's face was pale, and his head was covered with bandages. Two doctors were within call.

"Is that you, Dick Hamilton?" he asked in a weak voice.

"Yes. What do you want, Simon?" inquired Dick, softly, for the sight of Simon's sufferings banished all resentment.

"I'm afraid I'm badly hurt," went on Simon, "and I want to tell you something before—before I go away from here. Come closer."

"Now don't excite yourself," advised one of the doctors.

"I won't, but I must tell Dick," went on Simon. "I'm sorry I put up that game to steal Grit," he said, almost in a whisper. "But I needed money very much and I didn't see any other way to get it. Guy didn't have anything to do with it."

"I know," said Dick, softly.

"I played another mean trick on you," went on the injured youth. "I've been spying on you for Vanderhoof. After I got Grit and you saw me that day at the hotel, I was afraid. I knew Vanderhoof, or Colonel Dendon, as he sometimes calls himself, and I went to him. He said he could give me a job out West and he sent me here. Then, I guess it must have been the day you started, he telegraphed me to be on the lookout for you, and to inform Forty-niner Smith when you arrived. I did."

"Were you in the game to help work off a worthless mine on me?" asked Dick, a little resentfully.

"No, no," replied Simon, earnestly. "I only learned of that by accident. When I found out the mines were no good I was going to have nothing more to do with any of the gang. But Smith told me your father had once got the best of Vanderhoof in a business deal and that this was the only way they could get their money back—to sell him a worthless mine. They said it was done every day and—and I believed them. I only kept them informed of your movements so they could fix things up to—to deceive you, I suppose."

"Yes," assented Dick.

"But I'm done with 'em now," went on Simon. "I was riding out to the mine to-night, after I saw you three start for it. Oh, I kept close watch on you," he said in answer to Dick's look of surprise. "I started for the mine to warn them you were coming, as I knew they were going to do some 'salting.' My horse threw me before I'd gone far and—well, I'm pretty badly hurt, I guess."

"Now that will do," interrupted one of the physicians. "You can tell the rest another time. You must be quiet now."

"There isn't any more to tell," said Simon, in a whisper. "That's all, Dick, but I feel better for having told you."

"Well, Simon," said the millionaire's son, "I'm sorry you are hurt. I forgive you. I guess you didn't realize what you were doing."

"That's it. I never realized what bad men Vanderhoof, Smith and the others were. I'm done with them forever. I guess I can go to sleep now."

He turned over and closed his eyes. Dick softly left the room, followed by one of the doctors.

"Is he badly hurt?" he asked of the medical man, when they were out in the corridor.

"Well, he is hurt internally. I think we can pull him through with careful nursing. Is he a friend of yours?"

"I used to think he was," answered Dick. "I guess he got into bad company, that's the trouble. I'd like to help him if I could. Here, doctor, take this and see that he has good nursing, will you, please," and Dick thrust a hundred-dollar bill into the physician's hand.

"But this—this is quite a sum of money."

"Well, I guess dad would want me to spend it," replied Dick. "I've got lots more. Anyhow, I couldn't bear to think of Simon suffering, even if he did do me some mean turns. Will you look after him, doctor? I've got to go back East."

"I will, young man, and he can thank you for befriending him. I guess those men won't have anything more to do with him after this, and it's hard for a lad like him to be sick in a wild country like this. I'll see that he has the best of care."

Pondering over the strange events of the last few hours, Dick went back to his hotel. It was now nearly breakfast-time and he was ready for the meal, especially the hot coffee. Tim and Frank, also, did full justice to it, and then, being very sleepy, they went to bed, as did Dick.

"We'll start back home to-morrow," the millionaire's son said to his chums as he went to his room.

CHAPTER XXVII

THE PANIC

Although a little apprehensive that Smith and his gang might make trouble for him, Dick leisurely made his preparations for going back East, when, late in the afternoon, after a long slumber, he awoke much refreshed. But the miner and his men did not appear in Yazoo City. Dick called on the government assayer and told him what he and his chums had seen.

"That's a new way of 'salting' a mine," the official said. "A very good one, too, from a swindler's standpoint. Now, if you want to, you can make a complaint against those men and have them arrested."

"I'm afraid it wouldn't make the mines any good, or save the money dad and I put into them," said Dick.

"No, I don't believe it would. Besides, they are a slick crowd, I suppose, and you'd have trouble convicting them. Perhaps it is better to let it drop. I'll be on the watch, however, and if I hear of anyone about to invest in the stock of any mines Smith and his men are interested in I'll warn him."

Dick called to say good-bye to Simon. He found the bad boy a little improved, and when informed that he would be well taken care of the tears came into the eyes of the youth who had done so much to injure Dick.

"You—you're a brick!" he stammered. "I don't deserve it, but if—if I ever get well maybe I can do something for you."

"Oh, that's all right," replied Dick, somewhat affected by Simon's misery. "You'll soon be as well as ever, and when you do get around again, you'd better steer clear of such men as Colonel Dendon."

"I will," promised Simon, and he tried to return the pressure of Dick's hand, but it was hard work, for he was very weak.

Early the next morning Dick and his friends started for home. Dick was a little thoughtful, and Frank asked:

"Worrying about your lost money, Dick?"

"Well, not so much about the money as I am over the consequences. I counted on this mine investment being a good one. But, I have another. I guess my stock in the milk concern will pan out pretty well."

"If it don't youse had better come to N' York wid me, an' sell papes," advised Tim.

"I'll think of it," promised Dick, with a smile.

The ride back home was uneventful. Tim decided he would not go back to Hamilton Corners, as he was anxious to get to New York.

"Got to look after me paper business," he said, with a laugh. "I left me pardner in charge an' he's a little chap. Some of de big guys might drive him offen de swell corner we has. It's de best corner in N' York fer doin' business," he explained. "I stands in wid de cop on de beat an' he sees I ain't bothered. But I'm gittin' worried. I see some of de yellow journals is predictin' bad times an' I wants to be prepared for 'em. Besides, I've got some customers what owe me—one man run up a bill of a quarter jest 'fore I went on dat fresh-air racket, an' I want to collect it. So I t'ink I'll git back to little old N' York."

The boys parted from Tim with regret, for they liked his sterling character, which shone out through a coat of rough manners. He changed at a junction point for a train that went direct to the big city, and gaily waved his hand to them as it departed. He had profited much by coming to Hamilton Corners, for Dick had fitted him up with some good clothes, and, at parting, had slipped a bank bill into his hand.

Mr. Hamilton was glad to see his son back, and listened with interest to the account of the western trip.

"And so our money is gone," finished Dick.

"Well, there's no use crying over spilled milk, as the farmer's wife used to say," remarked the millionaire, with a calmness that Dick could not help envying. "It isn't the first time I've lost money by unwise speculation, but it's all in the game. I'm sorry for you, though, Dick."

"I'm sorry for myself. It looks as if I had a poor head for business."

"Oh, you'll learn," consoled his father. "It takes time."

"Yes, and there's Uncle Ezra waiting for me," went on Dick, as though he could see the harsh old man outside in a carriage, waiting to carry him off to the gloomy Firs. "When he hears of this he'll think sure I'm doomed to go and board with him."

"The year is quite a way from being completed," said Mr. Hamilton. "Lots of things may happen before your next birthday."

"I hope they do," said Dick, rather ruefully. "Anyway, I have my milk stock. They didn't send for another assessment while I was away, did they?"

"No, and I see the stock has advanced in value a point or two."

"Then I may be all right, after all. But I think I'll be on the lookout for another investment, and it's not going to be a gold mine, either," finished Dick.

It was about a week after this that, coming down to breakfast one morning, Dick was met by the butler.

"There's a gentleman waiting to see you, Master Dick," said the servant.

"To see me, Gibbs? Who is it?"

"I don't know, but he came very early and he says he has something to show you. He says he wants you to help him with it."

"Maybe it's another of those reporters," said Dick. "I will see him right after breakfast."

"I'd rather you see me now," interrupted a voice, and to Dick's astonishment there walked into the dining-room, from the library where he had been waiting, a little man, whose hair seemed to stick out at every point of the compass. His clothes were rather ragged, and, as he advanced, he kept running his hands through his hair. To do this he had to transfer, first from one arm to the other, a large box he carried.

"I'll not take much of your time," said the little man. "All I want is your assistance in having a lot of these machines made. You see how this one works," and, stooping over, he placed the box on the floor. From it came a clicking sound, as the little man, with his head tilted to one side, waited with watch in hand.

"It will go off in three minutes," he said.

Following the startling announcement of the little man Dick and Gibbs, the butler, seemed paralyzed. The room was so still that the ticking of the machine on the floor sounded like an immense alarm clock. Then, as the seconds passed and the stranger stood calmly looking alternately at Dick, Gibbs, and the box, the butler, with a sudden start back to life, exclaimed:

"Jump out of the window, Master Dick! I'll attend to this lunatic!"

"I'm not a lunatic!" shouted the little man. "I'm Professor Messapatomia!"

"Jump!" shouted Gibbs to Dick. "It isn't far to the ground. This thing will go off in a minute!"

"Half a minute," calmly corrected the stranger, as he snapped his watch shut. At that instant Mary, the waitress, came into the room with a large pitcher of water. As Dick turned to flee, for he realized that he might be courting death to remain, should the lunatic's infernal apparatus go off, Gibbs grabbed the pitcher.

"I'll fix it!" the butler cried, throwing the water at the ticking machine. "But jump, all the same, Master Dick!"

As Dick prepared to jump from one of the dining-room windows, believing that, as he had often read of such things occurring, he was to be made the victim of a crank, the machine gave a louder click. Professor Messapatomia, with a sudden motion of his arm, diverted the aim of Gibbs, and the water flew to one side of the box. At the same moment there was a jar, as from a heavy spring, and a shower of white objects scattered about the room.

"There!" exclaimed the professor, triumphantly, "that's how it works! Very simple, you see, and it scatters the bait all around. Then all you have to do is to take your pole and line and catch all the fish you want."

"Fish!" repeated Dick, somewhat in a daze. He had expected the house to be half-blown apart, yet the machine only scattered harmless pieces of paper about.

"Fish, of course," replied the professor, "What did you think this was?"

"Aren't you an Anarchist, and isn't that an infernal machine?" demanded Gibbs, wiping away some of the water he had accidentally spilled over his head when the professor knocked up his arm.

"Anarchist? Infernal machine?" repeated Professor Messapatomia. "Why, my dear sir, that is my latest invention of a fish-catching device. You see, you wind up the spring, and you set it to go off at any hour you wish. Then you put some finely chopped pieces of meat in this top pan. That is the bait. Only in this case, as I didn't want to muss up the room, I used bits of paper. At the proper time the machine, which you have set beside the stream where you desire to fish, goes off. The bait is thrown all over the surface of the water. It attracts the fish, and when you throw in your line you have no end of bites. It's the greatest idea of the age! It will revolutionize fishing! It's simply marvelous!

"I have just perfected the invention, but I need money to put the machine on the market. You, sir," turning to Dick, "are just the person to help me. I read of your immense wealth and that you are fond of all sports. Fishing is a sport, therefore I came to you. All I need is ten thousand dollars and it will make both of us rich in a year. Now, if you will kindly write me out a check for that amount, I'll bid you good-morning, and you can go on with your breakfast which I have interrupted."

He began to pick up the scattered bits of paper, Mary helping him, while Gibbs gazed rather stupidly at the queer figure with the bristling hair. Then Dick laughed.

"Well, you certainly gave me a scare," he said. "I thought you wanted to blow the place up. But I'm sorry I can't invest ten thousand dollars in that machine. It seems to me it would be just as easy to stand on the shore and throw the pieces of meat in the water by hand."

"Yes, of course, you could do it that way," admitted the professor, "but it isn't half so scientific. However, I'll not urge you," and, picking up his apparatus, he left the room after a low bow to Dick.

"He went away with less trouble than I expected," remarked Dick, as he looked at the wet place on the floor and at some of the bits of paper that still remained. "Well, Gibbs, I admit I was scared for a minute."

"So was I, Master Dick. I shouldn't have let him in, only you had given orders that all respectable-looking visitors were to be treated nicely, and I'm sure he looked respectable in spite of his queer hair."

"Oh, yes, he was respectable, all right. It's not your fault, Gibbs. I guess I'll have to draw the line about callers a little closer," concluded Dick as he sat down to breakfast.

The summer passed away and fall came. Dick returned to the academy, where he renewed his studies. Several times he was on the point of making another investment, but, as the stock of the milk company went up in value, he felt that this would answer the requirements of his mother's will, and furnish the profit called for. So, though he investigated many schemes that seemed to promise well, he did not take any stock in them.

It was in May of the following spring, when, having looked at a quotation of his milk stock, and found that it was a little higher than it had ever been before, Dick walked down to his father's bank to consult him about certain matters.

He found Mr. Hamilton in his private office, but the millionaire did not have a cheerful smile on his face. Instead he looked troubled.

"What's the matter, dad?" asked Dick.

"Well, I don't like the way the money market looks in New York," was the answer. "I've just heard by telegraph that several large banks have failed."

"Does it involve you?"

"To a certain extent, yes. Things look like a panic, such as we had a few years ago. Still, it may blow over."

"I wonder if it will affect the milk company?"

"It might. But there, Dick, don't go to worrying. You'll have enough of that to do when you get older. Things may turn out all right." But the worried look did not leave Mr. Hamilton's face, in spite of his attempt to cheer up his son.

The next morning when Dick came down to breakfast he saw his father at the table. But, instead of eating, the millionaire was eagerly looking at a newspaper. Dick glanced over his father's shoulder. There, staring at him, in big black letters, was the heading of a long article:

GREAT MONEY PANIC!

"Are things—are things in bad shape, dad?" asked Dick.

"Pretty much so," replied Mr. Hamilton, not looking up. "It's not as bad as I feared, though, and our bank will not suffer. However, lots of small concerns, and some big ones, have failed."

Then Dick caught sight of another part of the paper. He could hardly believe his eyes, for, in a prominent part of the page, was an article telling of the failure of the big milk concern in which he had invested.

"Dad!" he exclaimed, taking hold of the paper, and pointing to the account.

"Yes," replied Mr. Hamilton. "I saw it. Your investment is a failure, Dick."

CHAPTER XXVIII

HENRY IN TROUBLE

For a few moments father and son looked at each other. Dick hardly knew what to say, but the millionaire was evidently used to harder business disappointments than the present one, for he laughed and remarked:

"Never mind, Dick. You made a good attempt, but you failed. You have over a month yet in which to comply with the terms of the will. In that time you ought to be able to find some good, paying investment. Look over the paper. There's lots of bad financial news in it, but you may find some good. I must hurry to the bank. This panic will affect a number of our customers. I'm going to be very busy for some days to come."

Mr. Hamilton continued with his breakfast as if nothing had happened, but poor Dick's appetite vanished. He had counted so much on his shares in the milk company paying well that he had never thought of failure. Particularly as, of late, they had seemingly increased in value. But, as he learned by looking over the paper after his father left, many older and stronger concerns than the milk company in which he was interested had failed.

"Panics are bad things," murmured Dick, which sentiment was echoed by many another person that day.

Still Dick was not too much cast down. He knew he was a very wealthy young man, and he had no fear that his father's millions would be disturbed in the general hard times that would be sure to follow. But it hurt his pride that, with all his wealth, he could not do as much as little Tim Muldoon had done—start with nothing and make money.

"I'm almost ready to sell papers," mused Dick, with a smile.

However, he decided to do nothing rash. He still had more than a month until his birthday—the time limit for making the paying investment—and he felt that in that period something would occur that would enable him to fulfil the conditions of his mother's will.

"At any rate, I've got to go to school to-day," he said to himself, as he finished what, for him, was rather a slim breakfast. "I guess I'll come out right in the end. In fact, I've got to if I want to escape Uncle Ezra's clutches."

As Dick was coming home from his classes that afternoon, turning over in his mind various plans for making a good investment—from growing mushrooms or raising squabs to starting a brass band or becoming proprietor of a small circus—he saw coming toward him a dilapidated rig. He knew it could be none other than that of Henry Darby. As the horse and wagon approached it seemed to Dick to look, more than ever, ready to fall apart.

"Well, Henry," he remarked. "I see you're still in business. The panic hasn't bothered you, has it?"

"Not me, so much as it has the horse and wagon," replied Henry, with a laugh. "Don't you think that beast's ribs are nearer caving in than they were the last time you saw it?"

"He does look thinner, for a fact," admitted Dick.

"He is," and Henry spoke with solemn earnestness. "They were almost touching on either side this morning, but I gave him all the hay I could afford and that sort of spread them apart. As for the wagon—well, I don't need any bell or automobile horn to tell people I'm coming. It rattles enough to be heard two blocks off."

"Why don't you get a better outfit?" suggested Dick. "I should think it would pay."

"It might pay, but I couldn't. I'll have to get along with this for a while," and Henry looked at the odd assortment of old metal he had collected and was taking to his storage yard.

"Isn't the business paying as well as you thought it would, Henry?"

"Oh, the business is all right. The trouble is the way the president manages it," and Henry smiled ruefully. "You remember I told you dad had taken most of the surplus capital for one of his schemes," and he looked inquiringly at Dick.

"Yes, I remember, you said he thought there were thousands of dollars in it."

"Well, they're still there," said Henry, with dry humor. "Dad hasn't been able to induce 'em to come forth and nestle in his or my pockets. That's why I haven't enough money to buy a new horse and wagon. If I had it I could cover more ground in a day and do more business. As for this—this—well, I don't know what to call him. He reminds me of a heap of old iron, sticking out seven ways from Sunday, as the old saying is. You see his bones stick out like so many points."

"They do, for a fact," and Dick looked at the horse, that presented more angles than he had ever before imagined a horse possessed.

"There's one consolation," went on Henry. "He's cheap, but there's another disadvantage, he looks it. So does the wagon. Whenever I start away from home to collect old metal I always tell dad not to worry if I don't get back that night. There's no telling which will break down first—the horse or the wagon. It's like taking a voyage in a sailing ship, no telling when you'll arrive.

"Still," he went on, "there's one advantage. It keeps my journeys from being monotonous. Nothing like having a horse that may develop spavin, ring bone or heaves on the road any minute, or a wagon that may drop all four wheels at once and break every spring. It keeps me from getting lonesome."

"I'm sorry to hear the old metal business is so poor," remarked Dick. "What caused the trouble?"

"Well, dad got an idea that he knew a lot about old iron and such things. He started in to do the buying and I was to go after the stuff, when he had purchased it, and bring it home. He did buy some iron scrap and a lot of old horseshoes that I made a profit on. Then he heard of some metal at an old factory. Someone told him it had a lot of platinum in it. Now, platinum is very valuable. Dad thought he had struck a bargain. He paid a big price for the stuff. In fact, he used up every cent I had put away in order to get hold of that metal he thought had platinum in it."

"Didn't it?" asked Dick, as Henry stopped.

"Not a bit. Someone worked off a lot of steel and iron mixed, on poor old dad. I can't sell it anywhere. It's a peculiar mixture of metal. Some new company had it made for their machinery and they busted up. I've got the stuff back in the storage yard now. Can't get rid of it, though I've tried all over. That's where all my money is. So I have to begin all over again."

"It's too bad," said Dick, with ready sympathy.

"Yes, dad felt quite cut-up over it—for a few days. Then he thought of a new scheme. He says it'll make our fortune if he can only work it. But he hasn't any capital to start it, and, until I work some up in a small way, I haven't any, either. But there, I'm sorry I bothered you with all my troubles. I guess you have enough of your own. I'll pull out somehow." And calling to the horse, that had gone to sleep, Henry managed to arouse the animal and started off, the wagon rattling like a load of steel girders.

"Everything seems to be going wrong," murmured Dick, as he walked toward home. "I guess I'll have to help Henry along some more. He deserves it. And I must do something about my own investment. The time is getting shorter."

For two weeks Dick thought over many plans, but as fast as he made them he rejected them. Some his father advised him against, and others, after consideration, he decided would not give an adequate return for money invested. He was getting worried, for it was only a little more than a month until his birthday, when, if he had not complied with the provisions of the will, he must spend a year with his Uncle Ezra. The thought of that made him gloomy indeed.

He had almost decided, one afternoon, to put some money in a small ice-cream store, which he heard was being started at Lake Dunkirk for the summer excursion season.

"There ought to be good money in that," reasoned Dick. "I could get a lot of my friends to buy ice-cream there and it would help me to make a profit. I think I'll look up the manager and see if he'll take a partner."

He was about to go out, to put his newly-formed resolution into operation, when the maid announced a gentleman to see him.

"Who is it?" asked Dick.

"He won't tell me his name. He insists on seeing you at once."

"Another crank, I suppose. I thought they were done coming here. Well, show him in."

A moment later there entered the room a little man, with a long white beard and snow-white hair. He had the jolliest face imaginable, and looked just like a picture of Santa Claus.

"Allow me to introduce myself," he said, with a German accent. "I am Herr Wilhelm Doodlebrod, und I haf de airship at der freight station. When can I gif you an exhibition?"

"Airship?" murmured Dick, in bewilderment, While Herr Doodlebrod nodded several times and chuckled, as if it was the best joke in the world.

CHAPTER XXIX.

THE FLYING MACHINE.

Dick looked closely at Herr Doodlebrod, as if to see if the German had a bomb concealed about him, for the millionaire's son believed the man was another of the unfortunate persons who had some impossible scheme he wanted aid in perfecting.

"You vill like der airship, yes?" went on the smiling, little, old man. "Ah, he is a beautiful airship!—so strong, so graceful, und he sails along so just like a bird!"

Again he smiled, and then he laughed, as though he had just told Dick a very funny story. The German's good nature was catching, and Dick also smiled.

"I'm afraid I don't quite understand you," the boy said.

"Ach! Dot is easy!" replied Herr Doodlebrod. "See, listen, it is dis vay. I am de greatest inventor of an airships vot efer vas," and he said it as if he meant it, with child-like directness, "I haf der ship vot all der scientists haf long been vaiting for. I haf bring him to your town und I show you how he vorks."

"But why did you bring it to me?" asked Dick.

"Vhy? Because, listen," and the little man approached closer and began whispering. "I read about you in der papers. Iss it nod so?" and he smiled broadly. "You are der richest young man vot efer vos. Ach, I know!" and he winked one eye at Dick, as though the millionaire's son had tried to conceal something.

"So, now I proceed. I hear of your great wealth. I learn you vos a young mans. You are bright, quick, smart. Yes, iss it not? Vell, I invent der airships. I am a shoemaker in my city, many miles from here. Vun day der great ideas comes to me. I see a bat fly. Quick, I say, I will make me a airships like der bat. He is heavier as a bird, yet he flies. So I stop making shoes und I make airships. Iss it not so?" and once more the smile illuminated the kindly face.

"Did you succeed?" asked Dick.

"Not at first," replied the German, gravely. "Many, many times I t'ink I fly into der air, but I falls to der ground. Sometimes it hurts. Vunce I breaks my leg. But dot iss noddings. Ven I get vell I make improvements. Now I haf der great machine vot flies; yes?"

"Where is it?" asked Dick, becoming interested in the queer little man.

Then Herr Doodlebrod proceeded to explain. He said he had heard of Dick's wealth, and, needing money to make some improvements in his ship, he had taken it apart, shipped it to Hamilton Corners, and followed the machine. The airship was now at the freight station, he added, and he was about to put it together and give a demonstration.

"What for?" asked Dick.

"To show you how he vorks. Den you vill believe. You vill invest some money in it, I shall make der improvements, get a better motor, und ve win der government prize of ten thousand dollars."

"Government prize?" repeated Dick.

The German explained at greater length. The United States Government, in common with other nations, recognizing the future in flying machines for war purposes, had established a sort of competitive test, with a substantial prize for the machine which successfully fulfilled the conditions. The chief ones were that the apparatus must move through the air at a certain distance above the ground, must carry two passengers, must be under perfect control, and must stay up a certain length of time. The German said his machine answered nearly all these requirements, but that he needed some new materials in it, and, more than anything else, a new motor. He had used up all his savings and had tried in vain to get someone to help him. So, hearing of Dick, he had decided to appeal to the millionaire's son.

"It iss not so much dot I need," he went on. "If I had five hundred dollars it would be enough. My dear young frient, I appeal to you. I do not ask you for dot moneys. I say just invest it in my machine und ve vill be successful und get der ten thousand dollars. You shall haf five thousand. Iss not dot a good investment?"

A sudden idea came to Dick. An investment, promising quick returns was just what he needed. He had tried in vain to find one, and the time was daily growing shorter. Here might be the very chance he desired. But there was one important thing. He must be sure that the airship would fly. If it did not the prize would not be won and he would be out five hundred dollars. Herr Doodlebrod saw the doubt pictured on Dick's face.

"I do not ask you to take my word," he said, gravely. "I only ask for a chance to show you. See, I vill bring my machine here. I vill put him togeder und I vill fly in him. Der trouble iss dot I cannot go far enough or stay up long enough vid der motor dot I haf. Wid a new vun I can. I need der money for der new motor. Vill you invest it?"

"I will!" exclaimed Dick, suddenly.

"Ach! Bless you, my young friend!" and Herr Doodlebrod rushed over to the millionaire's son and threw his arms about Dick, an embrace somewhat difficult to escape from, so hearty was it.

"But I must first talk to my father," went on Dick, when Herr Doodlebrod's enthusiasm had somewhat cooled down. "If the ship is a success so far, and by investing five hundred dollars a better one can be entered for the prize, so that I can win part of it, I'm sure he would have no objections."

"I go for my airship," said the German. "I bring him here und in two days he is ready to fly."

"Better not bring it here," advised Dick. "There isn't much room to try it around the house, and too big a crowd would gather. We'll go off in the country somewhere. My father owns some property about five miles from here. It's a big level field, and I think that will be the best place."

"Der very t'ing," assented the German, and Dick told him how to get to it. Herr Doodlebrod hurried off to the freight station to arrange for having his dismantled flying machine brought to the place where the test was to be made.

"This may be the very thing I've been looking for," reasoned Dick. "Winning five thousand dollars on an investment of five hundred is pretty good. I guess that will fulfill the conditions of mother's will. The question is: will it fly? But if it doesn't at the first test I'm out nothing. And if it flies with his present engine it surely will with a better one. I must tell dad about it."

Mr. Hamilton was not much impressed with Herr Doodlebrod's plan. He admitted that the government had offered a prize for a successful airship, but he thought an old shoemaker was hardly a possible person to win it.

"Scientific men have devoted many years of study to the problem," he said, "and they have not solved it yet. Still, of course, there's a chance. As you say, you're out nothing if it doesn't work the first time. But how about after you have put the five hundred dollars in, and the ship doesn't sail?"

"If it sails with the old engine it surely ought to with the new," declared Dick, repeating his favorite argument.

Mr. Hamilton consented that Dick might make the investment. It was a queer one, he said, but he agreed that if Herr Doodlebrod won the prize, and gave Dick half, the terms of Mrs. Hamilton's will would have been complied with.

"I'll get out of going to Uncle Ezra's yet," said the millionaire's son. "The mine failed, the milk company failed, but the airship will beat them all."

Herr Doodlebrod was a quick worker. In less time than Dick had believed possible he had the parts of the machine at the place decided on for the test. There, under the inventor's directions, men aided him in putting it together.

In shape it looked like a huge bat, and was built on the principle of an aeroplane. At the stern an immense rudder was turned by a small gasolene motor, and there were several smaller rudders for directing the course of the apparatus. There was a little car, of basket-work, amidships, where the operator sat.

It was three days before the German was satisfied that all was in readiness for the preliminary test that was to tell if Dick would spend five hundred dollars on improvements. In spite of the attempt to keep the matter quiet the news leaked out, and a big crowd gathered to see Herr Doodlebrod make an attempt to fly.

"I do not promise so much to-day," he said, as he saw that all was in readiness. "I vill go up, circle about for a vile, und den I haf to come down. My engine iss not powerful enough. But vid der new one! Ach, den ve vill fly far und vin der prize!"

He climbed into the little basket-car. Giving a look over the various handles and levers, and seeing that all was clear ahead, Herr Doodlebrod started the motor. It began to revolve rapidly, crackling like a battery of Gatling guns.

"Now I fly!" exclaimed the German, as he threw on the clutch that operated the propeller. The big airship trembled as the massive blades whizzed through the air, and all eyes were fixed on it to detect the moment when it might leave the earth and sail aloft.

CHAPTER XXX

A DISASTROUS FLIGHT

"There it goes!" cried a score of voices, Dick's among them. And, sure enough, the airship moved. Slowly, but gathering speed, like some ungainly creature, it rose into the air in a slanting direction. Up and up it went, until it was about two hundred feet above the earth. Then Herr Doodlebrod shifted a rudder and the machine flew along on a level keel.

"Look at her go!" cried Frank Bender, for he and all of Dick's boy chums had been invited to the test. "Gee, but I wish I was in her!"

"You'd stand on your head on one of the propeller blades, I suppose," commented Walter Mead.

"Look, he's turning around!" exclaimed Frank, to change the subject from his acrobatic abilities, concerning which he was a bit sensitive.

Sure enough, Herr Doodlebrod was flying around in a circle. He seemed to be able to manage the ship perfectly, and Dick was delighted. He already saw the prize won with the improved craft, and himself holder of half the money.

"Look out, he's falling!" yelled Bricktop, suddenly, and the crowd of men, women, boys and girls strained their eyes to see what was happening. The airship was certainly coming down.

"Oh, he'll be killed! Isn't it terrible!" exclaimed Birdy Lee, who, with some of her girl friends, had come to watch the test.

"I'm going to faint!" declared Nettie Henderson, covering her eyes with her hands.

"No, he isn't falling; he's steering it down!" declared Dick. "He's all right!"

This announcement relieved the feelings of all. Herr Doodlebrod was indeed coming down. But he had his ship under perfect control, as shown by the manner in which he steered it in a half circle so as to return to the place from which he had started. In a few minutes he allowed it to come to a stop on the ground, in the midst of the throng, where it alighted as gently as a bird.

"Vot I tell you?" he asked of Dick, triumphantly. "I could haf stayed longer, but my engine he vill not stand it. Ven ve gets der new motor—den ve two vill sail in der clouds."

"I guess you'll have to excuse me from the first trip," objected Dick, with a smile. "I want to see it tried first."

"It iss as safe as on der ground. Vait, I vill show you. But now, are you satisfied?"

"Yes," replied Dick. "I'm willing to invest five hundred dollars in a new motor. Then we'll see how she works."

"Und den ve vin der grand prize," announced the German. "But I haf much to do. Ven can you spare der money?"

"As soon as you want it. Perhaps you had better come back to town with me and we can talk it over with my father."

The airship was taken to a big barn near the scene of the test and some workmen left in charge to guard it from the curious crowd that gathered. Herr Doodlebrod was as calm and collected as though flying was an every-day accomplishment of his, but Dick was quite excited over what had taken place. Not only did he see the conditions of his mother's will fulfilled, but he was glad of the opportunity of taking part in helping to solve the problem of aerial navigation.

Mr. Hamilton was informed of the test and its success. A form of agreement was drawn up to protect the interests of all parties, and Dick gave Herr Doodlebrod a check for five hundred dollars, taking a mortgage on the machine as security, a proposition the inventor himself suggested.

"Now I go to New York for der engine," he announced.

Three days later a letter arrived from the German. He said he was having some difficulties in getting the engine made, but expected to be back at Hamilton Corners in a week.

"You'll have to hustle, Dick, to win that prize before the year expires," said his father, with a smile. "Aren't you getting anxious?"

"A little, but I guess it will all come out right. It won't take long to install the engine once we get it."

At the end of the week the German arrived with the engine. He was enthusiastic over it, and declared the government prize was already his. He had communicated with a representative of the War Department, who promised to be on hand when the test was made, to see if Herr Doodlebrod's machine answered the requirements.

"But haf no fears," boasted the inventor to Dick. "It vill, und ve vill reap der reward."

"I hope so," answered Dick. "I haven't much time left."

There were several delays in getting the ship in shape for the decisive test. Herr Doodlebrod was not satisfied with one of the rudders and ordered a new one made. Dick urged haste, as he had in mind the year limit fixed in his mother's will.

"Easy, easy," counseled the German. "I haf spent fifteen years on der machine; vot iss a few days?"

"Much, to me," said Dick.

"Do not vorry, my young friend," comforted the inventor. "You shall haf made der finest investment vot effer vos. I, Herr Doodlebrod, say so. Dot uncle of yours shall nefer get you." For Dick had told the German about the conditions of the will.

But, in spite of all their haste, it was some time longer ere the machine was ready for the test. The new motor had been put in, and, though it was not tried in the air, worked perfectly. The propeller revolved twice as fast, and this, the inventor said, meant twice as much speed.

"To-morrow ve haf der test," announced the German one evening, as he completed the last change on the airship.

"Will the government official be here?" asked Dick.

"He has promised. I go to bed early dot my nerves may be in good shape. Haf no fears, I vill fly, und fly far. Der requirements vill all be met; I, Herr Doodlebrod, say so."

True to his promise, the government expert on aerial matters arrived at Hamilton Corners the next day. He sought out Herr Doodlebrod and Dick, and said he was ready to see their machine tested. The preparations had all been made and there was no delay.

In Dick's runabout he, his father, the inventor and the representative from the War Department, Colonel Claflin, went out to the big field where the airship awaited them. A large crowd was waiting. It seemed that everyone in Hamilton Corners, who could, by any possibility get away from work, was there.

The airship was hauled from the barn where it had been during the night, closely guarded against possible accidents. It looked larger than ever as, almost at the last minute, the inventor had increased the size of some of the bat-like wings that extended on either side.

Herr Doodlebrod was the calmest person in the big crowd. He went about looking at the wheels, levers, rods, rudders and the propeller as if he was merely a spectator. But his sharp eyes did not miss anything. He detected a loose screw in the motor and called for a tool to adjust it. Then, having seen that the gasolene tank was filled, and that the various handles for controlling the machine worked smoothly, he took his place in the basket-car, which had been enlarged.

"Vould you not like to come?" he asked of Dick. But Dick shook his head in dissent.

"You come," the inventor invited Colonel Claflin, but the government representative begged to be excused.

"I may try it with you after your first flight," he said.

As the specifications called for the carrying of two passengers the absence of one was made up by some bags of sand to give the necessary weight.

"Iss all clear?" asked Herr Doodlebrod.

"Clear she is," replied his chief helper.

"Den here I goes!" exclaimed the inventor as he started the motor and threw in the clutch operating the propeller.

The big arms beat the air and hummed shrilly as they whizzed around. The new motor made the frail airship tremble. There was a moment's hesitation, as if the craft hated to leave the earth, and then, with a little jerk, it soared aloft.

"Hurrah!" yelled the crowd.

"She works! She works!" cried Dick, capering about in delight. He thought the prize already won. Even Colonel Claflin looked pleased.

Herr Doodlebrod deflected one of the rudders and the airship went up at a sharp angle. In a few seconds it was several hundred feet high. Then it started to move about in a circle.

"Wonderful!" murmured several.

"He seems to know his business," remarked Mr. Hamilton. "I didn't believe it would work. I haven't much faith in airships."

"Well, it has gone, so far," replied Colonel Claflin. "But the test is not completed. Let's watch him."

In a great circle Herr Doodlebrod sent his ship around. He turned and twisted this way and that. Then he set off in a straight line, as called for by the government requirements.

But suddenly something happened. There was a sharp sound, like an explosion, up on the airship. The big propellor was seen to fly to pieces and come fluttering down, a mass of twisted wire and cloth.

Then came another ominous sound. It was a louder explosion, and a sheet of fire was seen to envelop the ship.

"His gasolene tank has gone up!" exclaimed Colonel Claflin. "He'll be killed!"

The airship seemed rent apart. The two big, bat-like wings soared off to one side. Rudders, wheels, levers and parts of machinery came raining down. The bat wings settled to the earth more slowly.

"Where is the inventor?" asked Mr. Hamilton. "Has he been blown to pieces?"

"It looks so," replied the colonel. "Poor chap! I'm afraid he didn't know so much about airships as he thought."

There came a cry from the crowd, not a cry of horror, but of wonder. The colonel, Dick and Mr. Hamilton looked toward where they pointed.

There, falling through space from his wrecked airship, was Herr Doodlebrod.

CHAPTER XXXI

GOOD NEWS—CONCLUSION

"Look! Look!" cried the crowd, again and again.

And there was no small cause for wonder; for, though the inventor was falling to earth, he had hold of one of the immense bat-like wings. It acted exactly as a parachute, the air catching under the curved surface. Thus the inventor came down so slowly that he was not in the slightest danger. It was a wonderful escape.

No sooner had he alighted than he hurried up to where Dick stood, his face showing the sorrow he felt.

"Vell, my young friend," said Herr Doodlebrod, "ve haf made vun grand mistake. But I know vat der trouble vas. I need a stronger propellor. Ve vill make vun at vunce, und haf anodder test."

"I'm afraid it will be too late for me," remarked Dick, ruefully.

"Ach, dot iss so," assented the German. "But neffer mind. I shall yet fly. I vill at once proceed to build a new machine. I vill make some more shoes until I haf saved money enough, und den I try again," and he smiled as though what had just happened was the thing he had always desired.

The crowd gathered about the disabled airship, which was mostly consumed by the flames before it had reached the earth. Herr Doodlebrod had the men save what they could, and, not a bit discouraged, he set about packing up the remnants to take away.

"Too bad," remarked Colonel Claflin, "but such accidents will happen. He's a cool fellow, at any rate."

Dick and his father went home together in the runabout, the colonel declining their invitation to pay them a visit. The German inventor went away and that was the last seen of him.

Swiftly the days passed, and in sheer desperation Dick invested several hundred dollars in three different schemes. But none of them paid. In one he lost all his money and in the others he got his money back and that was all.

"It's no use!" he groaned to himself. "I guess it takes a brighter fellow than I to make money."

Mr. Hamilton did not say much, but he was almost as anxious as his son, for he did not wish to see Dick fail.

One morning Mr. Hamilton went out with Dick in the youth's runabout.

"Well, my son, to-morrow is your birthday," remarked the parent, after speaking of many things in general.

"I know it, dad," was the gloomy answer. And then Dick went on: "I suppose there is no way of getting clear of the provisions of that will?"

"I know of none. Your dear departed mother's wishes must be respected."

"Oh, dear!" Dick gave a long sigh. "Well, perhaps I can stand Uncle Ezra, but it's going to be a—er—a stiff proposition."

"I'm sorry," commented Mr. Hamilton. "But perhaps it will be a good thing for you. Your Uncle Ezra has excellent discipline, and he's a good man of business."

"I don't doubt that, dad."

Father and son did not say much during the ride home, as each was busy with his thoughts. As Dick went up the steps of the Hamilton mansion the butler met him at the door.

"Your Uncle Ezra is here," he announced.

"Oh, dear!" commented Dick, with a groan.

"Ah, Nephew Richard," was Mr. Larabee's greeting when Dick found him in the library. "I've come to pay *you* a little visit, you see. I happened to remember that to-morrow is your birthday, and, according to the—to the provisions of your mother's will you may be going to pay *me* a visit. I can't say I altogether approve of that will, still we will not discuss that now. The main thing is, Have you made the paying investment called for?"

"No, I haven't, Uncle Ezra."

"Hum, well, I didn't think you would. Boys have no head for business nowadays. I knew your money would do you little good. So you are to come and live a year with me, eh?"

"I suppose so. Yes, of course, Uncle Ezra," and Dick tried to make his voice sound cheerful, but it was hard work when he thought of the gloomy house.

"Well, I told Samanthy I'd bring you back with me, and she's going to have your room all ready. Then, too, I've arranged to send you to a good boarding school. It is taught by a friend of mine; a man who doesn't believe in nonsense."

Dick could see, in fancy, the kind of a school Uncle Ezra would pick out, and he could also fancy the principal of it, a harsh, stern old man. He sighed, but there was no help for it.

"So I will take you away with me to-morrow," went on Mr. Larabee, rubbing his hands as if delighted at the prospect. "I shall—Gracious goodness! What's that?" he exclaimed, jumping from his chair, as a loud growl sounded from under the library table. "Have you a wild animal in here, Nephew Richard?"

"I guess it's my bulldog, Grit," replied Dick. "Here, Gibbs," calling the butler, "have Grit taken to the stable."

Grit was led away, growling out a protest.

"I can't bear dogs," said Uncle Ezra. "You'll not be allowed to have one at The Firs, so you had better get rid of this one."

"Oh, I suppose I can leave Grit home," answered Dick, with a sigh. "Can I get you something to eat, Uncle Ezra?" he asked, trying to be hospitable.

"No, thank you, Nephew Richard. I never eat between meals, nor do I allow it at my house. Three times a day is enough to eat."

"Maybe you would like some lemonade; it's quite warm to-day." Dick was both hungry and thirsty.

"No, lemonade is bad for the liver, I have heard. You may get me some plain water, if you please."

"And I've got to live a year with him," mused Dick as he went out to get his uncle a drink. "Why, oh why, didn't some of my investments succeed?"

Dick spent a miserable evening with his uncle. Mr. Hamilton came home from the bank, whither he had gone after the ride, and greeted his brother-in-law.

"Well, I guess you'll have to take Dick back with you," said the millionaire, with an attempt at cheerfulness.

"I intend to, and when he comes back from living with me he'll be a different lad," said Mr. Larabee, grimly.

"I guess that's true enough," thought Dick.

He dreamed that night that he went to his uncle's house in an airship, and when they got there it turned into a vault in a cemetery and he was made a prisoner in it. He awoke with a start to find his uncle calling to him from the hall outside his door.

"Come, Nephew Richard," said Mr. Larabee. "It's six o'clock, and you'll have to get up early when you're at my house. Might as well begin now."

"Oh, this is a beautiful birthday," said Dick, with a groan, as he began to dress. "Six o'clock! Ugh!"

It was arranged that they were to take an early train to Dankville, and, soon after breakfast, Dick, having packed his suitcase, and arranged to have his trunk forwarded to him at The Firs, went to the library where his father and uncle were waiting for him.

"Well, Dick," remarked Mr. Hamilton, with a little catch in his voice, for he hated to part with his son, though he knew the experience might be good for him. "I guess it's time to say good-bye."

"I suppose so," replied Dick, trying to keep back the tears, which, in spite of all he could do, would come to his eyes.

"Yes, we must be going," agreed Mr. Larabee. "I'll write to you, Mortimer, and let you know how Dick gets along. I have no doubt but I'll make a fine man of him. Too much wealth is bad for a young man. Come along, Nephew Richard."

Dick started to leave the room. At that instant the doorbell rang and Gibbs, answering it, came into the library and announced:

"Mr. Henry Darby and his son, to see Mr. Dick."

"I guess they have come to say good-bye," said the millionaire's son. "Show them in, Gibbs."

"Hank" Darby did not need any "showing." He was in the library as Gibbs turned to go back to the door.

"Excuse this intrusion," he began, "but I am in a hurry. I have a very important scheme on and I must attend to it at once. But my son insisted that we come and tell Mr. Dick what has happened, he being a partner in our enterprise—The International and Consolidated Old Metal Corporation."

"Yes, Dick!" cried Henry, unable to wait for his father to tell the news in his slow, pompous way. "Things are in fine shape. In fact the old metal business can now pay a dividend."

"A dividend?"

"Yes, you remember me telling you about a lot of old scrap-iron and steel dad bought, thinking it had platinum in it?"

"Yes, and it didn't have any in."

"Merely an error in judgment," murmured Mr. Darby. "Any business man, with large schemes on hand, is liable to make them."

"Well, while the metal didn't have any platinum in it, it had a peculiar quality of steel. It is very valuable, and I—that is we"—turning toward his father—"have just sold it to a large firm that wants it to make some very fine springs with."

"Yes, the deal is just completed," broke in Mr. Darby. "My judgment in that old metal is confirmed. I have accepted an offer of two thousand dollars for it. Under the terms of the incorporation papers one-half of that goes to Dick. I now take pleasure in handing you my check for that amount, as president of The International and Consolidated Old Metal Corporation," and with a grand air "Hank" handed Dick a slip of paper.

"Is this mine?" asked the millionaire's son, in some bewilderment.

"It is," replied Mr. Darby. "It is part of the return from your investment of two hundred and fifty dollars which you put into the firm of which I am president, you treasurer, and my son secretary and general manager."

"That is, I collect the old iron and sell it," explained Henry, seeing that Mr. Larabee looked puzzled. "Dick was kind enough to invest some money with our company last year, and I am glad I can make a return for him—or, rather, dad can, for he bought the metal that turned out so valuable."

"Then—then—" began Dick, a light slowly breaking over him, "without intending it, I have made a good, paying investment. A thousand dollars for two hundred and fifty is good, isn't it, dad?"

"Fine, I would say," cried Mr. Hamilton, with a smile.

"And this is my birthday! The year is just up!" went on Dick. "I—I won't have to go and live with Uncle——"

He stopped in some confusion.

"Do you mean to tell me that this is a bona-fide investment, Mortimer?" asked Mr. Larabee, turning to his brother-in-law.

"Perfectly legal and legitimate," interrupted Mr. Darby. "Here is a copy of the incorporation agreement."

"Well," remarked Uncle Ezra, with a disappointed air, "I suppose you have fulfilled the conditions of your mother's will, Nephew Richard. I congratulate you," and he shook hands rather stiffly.

"Well, who would have thought it?" gasped Dick, hardly able to believe his good fortune. "I never gave that investment a thought—in fact, I never considered it an investment, Henry."

"It was, all the same, and I'm glad I am able to do you a favor, for you did me a mighty good turn. The old metal business is in fine shape, and I have more than I can attend to."

"Yes, we must be going, I have a big scheme on hand," put in Mr. Darby. "A very big scheme, there are enormous possibilities in it. *Enormous*, sir!"

"If they only come out," said Henry, with a laugh, as he and his father withdrew.

"Well, if you are not to come back with me, I suppose I may as well be going," remarked Uncle Ezra, after a pause. "Samanthy will be looking for me. I'll say good-bye."

He turned to go, and at that instant an ominous growl came from under the library table.

"What's that?" asked Mr. Larabee in alarm.

"I—I think it's Grit," replied Dick, trying not to laugh.

"That bulldog again!" exclaimed Mr. Larabee. "I hate dogs! I wish——"

But what he wished he never said, for Grit, seeming to know that an enemy of his master was present, rushed from under the table, and, with opened mouth, though he probably would not have bitten him, rushed at Uncle Ezra.

"Here, Grit!" cried Dick. "Come back here this instant!"

But, with a wild yell, Mr. Larabee ran from the room, followed by the dog. Out through the hall and down the steps Dick's uncle ran, the dog growling behind him. But Gibbs captured Grit at the front door and held him.

"Grit! Aren't you ashamed of yourself?" asked Dick, trying not to laugh. But Grit growled in a way that seemed to say he was not in the least ashamed.

Mr. Larabee hurried off down the street, not once looking back.

"Well, that was a narrow escape," murmured Dick. "Eh, dad?"

"I suppose so. Still a visit to your uncle's house might have done you good," added the millionaire, with a twinkle in his eyes.

"Now, dad," went on Dick, "I suppose that as I have fulfilled all the conditions of the will I may do pretty nearly as I please."

"Not altogether," and the millionaire spoke rather gravely. "It is true you will have a certain control of your money left you by your mother, but you remember I told you, a year ago, there were certain other provisions of the will. One of them is that you attend a good military school."

"A military school!" exclaimed Dick, his eyes sparkling. "That will be fine."

"Yes, but wait. The conditions are that you attend there and become popular with the students in spite of your wealth. In short, that you make your own way up without the aid of your millions, and become one of the upper classmen through your own efforts. It is not going to be as easy as you think, but I trust you can do it. There is no great hurry about it. I will give you a few months of leisure and then you must get ready for a new life."

"Oh, dad, I think it will be fine!" exclaimed Dick; "I've always wanted to go to a military academy!" But he little knew of what was in store for him. Those who wish to follow the further adventures of the young millionaire will find them set forth in the second volume of this series, entitled "Dick Hamilton's Cadet Days; or the Handicap of a Millionaire's Son."

"Well, Grit, you certainly routed Uncle Ezra," said Dick, as he patted the ugly head of his pet. "I don't know as I blame you. But it's all over now, though I had some stirring times while it lasted." And, whistling gaily, Dick went out to deposit in the bank his thousand-dollar check, the profits of his one paying investment.

End of the book.